The complet Mediterranean diet Cookbook for Beginners:

Enjoy Combine budget-friendly recipes: 2000+ days of Easy & Healthy Robust in Flavor dishes. 60-day meal plan for lifelong healt included.

Lisa Mckeith

Table of Contents

INTRODUCTION

Welcome to "Mediterranean Eats," your passport to the sunny flavors and heart-healthy benefits of Mediterranean cuisine. In this cookbook, we embark on a culinary journey across the Mediterranean, bringing you 120 unique and delicious recipes inspired by the rich traditions of this region. Get ready to savor the flavors of the Mediterranean and adopt a healthier and more dynamic lifestyle.

What is the Mediterranean diet?

The Mediterranean Diet is a nutritional model widespread in some countries of the Mediterranean basin and represents the set of eating habits that have developed over the millennia, constituting a unicum for wealth in biodiversity. It was introduced by the American physiologist Ancel Keys, who, observing the population of some areas of southern Italy and noting its particular longevity, decided to study its habits, investigating the effects on the epidemiological incidence of cardiovascular diseases, tumors, and chronic diseases, such as obesity and diabetes II, related to nutrition.

Based on the study, the first example of the Food Pyramid of the Mediterranean Diet was developed for the first time in 1980. The population observed by Keys was represented to a large extent by farmers, with a very low socio-economic level, which is why their diet was rich above all in products from the earth. The Mediterranean diet consists of a greater supply of carbohydrates (especially bread and pasta), which cover 55% of the calorie intake; the contribution of simple sugars is, however, reduced and represented to a large extent by fruit. Fats are moderately present and represent 30% of total calories and have an abundant monounsaturated component, being mainly represented by olive oil. Proteins are the least present in the diet, and their share reaches a maximum of 15%; they are mainly of plant origin and, to a lesser extent, of animal origin. The latter derive from fish, followed by white meats, eggs, dairy products, and red meats. The concept of the "Mediterranean lifestyle" also contemplates adequate physical activity, understood as regular, sufficient, and continuous exercise, adequate rest, conviviality, respect for seasonality, and frugality.

The Main Features

The traditional Mediterranean Diet that is consumed by the populations of the Mediterranean basin in the immediate aftermath of the war, that is, in the 50-60s, is not only a way of eating but a set of knowledge, social habits, and cultural traditions historically handed down by the populations bordering the Mediterranean Sea therefore, rather than diet understood as a restrictive or limiting regime, one can speak of one "Lifestyle "whose importance was recognized worldwide by UNESCO, which in November 2010 recognized the Mediterranean Diet as" intangible heritage of humanity."

The decision is based on the recognition that: "this simple and frugal way of eating meals has favored intercultural contacts and conviviality over time, giving life to a formidable body of knowledge, social customs and traditional celebrations of many Mediterranean populations."

A single definition of the Mediterranean Diet is not easy, given that in the Mediterranean area, countries with different cultural backgrounds coexist, different ethnic and religious roots, different social and economic statuses, and different agricultural production, which involve different food choices.

In fact, there is no single "Mediterranean Diet" but a common dietary pattern, "Mediterranean," which has these main characteristics. These characteristics include the following:

- An abundance of foods of vegetable origin (vegetables, vegetables, fresh and dried fruit, legumes, bread, and pasta from non-reconstituted wholemeal flour and other whole grains such as barley, spelled, and oats, which ensure both a low Glycemic Index and a balancing and satiating role);
- Prevalent consumption of fresh and seasonal food, almost always of local origin and therefore at zero kilometer;
- Use of olive oil as the main source of fats;
- Pesce, white meat, and eggs from free-range hens are consumed a few times a week;

- Daily but moderate consumption of cheeses and milk yogurt from grazing animals, rich in omega-3 fatty acids and antioxidant vitamins;

- Low consumption of red meat (it was consumed only on Sundays by the wealthiest families and occasionally by the less wealthy families when farmyard and work animals were sacrificed because they were no longer able to give an income);

- Regular use of aromatic herbs that allow you to create a diet of excellent flavor and great palatability, reducing the need to use salt and fatty condiments in excessive quantities;

- Moderate wine intake with meals;

- Redottissimo consumption of sweets, which were consumed only on the occasion of family and patronal feasts.

In relation to health, the concept of the "Mediterranean lifestyle" is characterized by adequate physical activity, understood as regular, sufficient, and continuous.

What are the Nutrients at the Base of the Mediterranean diet?

The nutrients contained in foods corresponding to Mediterranean dietary habits are:

- Few proteins and mainly of vegetable origin;

- Carbohydrates with low index and glycemic load, with simple sugars almost absent;

- High monounsaturated/saturated fatty acids ratio;

- Quantity and omega-3 / omega-6 fatty acid ratio much greater than that of our day's diet, which tends to unity;

- Beta carotene, tocopherols, abundant vitamin C;

- High polyphenols (which make the Mediterranean Diet a functional diet);

- Calcium, magnesium, and potassium high;

- Sodio bass

The Mediterranean Diet is also a predominantly raw food diet; almost all dishes are cooked at low temperatures for a long time, and many foods and condiments, especially olive oil, are added to raw dishes and are, therefore, also a low AGE (Advanced Glycation End-products) diet. Extensive literature indicates that AGEs are dangerous molecules for the body because they have effects related to inflammation and aging and their involvement in the pathogenesis of numerous degenerative diseases.

AGEs are the products of the most advanced stages of the non-enzymatic glycation reaction of proteins. This phenomenon takes place both in the body and in foods subjected to treatments, particularly physico-chemicals (e.g., high temperatures and low humidity). Therefore, there is a share of endogenous AGE and one of dietary origin that contribute to the progressive accumulation of AGE in the tissues.

Almost all foods produced through industrial processes are very rich in AGE, not only because of the high temperature but also because of the processing methods used, capable of altering the chemical nature of the substances involved. Even in the domestic environment, it is possible to treat food so that it contains a greater or lesser quantity of glycation products: scorching, roasting, and toasting means forming AGE.

The Mediterranean Diet as a Lifestyle

The Mediterranean diet is much more than just a food. It promotes social interaction since the common meal is the basis of social customs and holidays shared by a given community. It has given rise to a considerable body of knowledge, songs, maxims, tales, and legends. The diet is based on respect for the territory and biodiversity and guarantees the conservation and development of traditional activities and trades related to fishing and agriculture in Mediterranean communities".

These were the reasons that in November 2010 led to the recognition of the Mediterranean Diet as an intangible cultural heritage of humanity. A heritage that recognizes the food traditions and lifestyle of those peoples overlooking the Mediterranean (Italy, Spain, Greece, Morocco, Portugal, Croatia, and Cyprus).

Traditions that have been handed down from generation to generation refer not only to a simple list of foods but to a real philosophy and a lifestyle, to social models that aim to build and strengthen interpersonal relationships, creating a constant and constructive dialogue but also an extraordinary endless creativity. This is how the community's values and identity are handed down, creating that strong and important bond that derives from recognition and belonging and, of course, from continuity. But above all, they testify to the vitality of the culture in which it is born and developed because food has been culture foreverand everywhere.

Seven Steps Towards Natural Health

These seven steps are vital if you want to live a long and healthy life. With them, you can heal "incurable diseases" such as cancer, diabetes, heart disease, and others naturally, without medications, surgery, or chemotherapy. Do your best to follow them all, and keep in mind that there is also an optional eighth that recommends prayer or meditation.

1. See an American macrobiotic diet based on whole grains. Nutrition is the most important factor in enjoying good health. A proper diet heals diseases. Everything else is secondary.

2. Take proven supplements to accentuate the effects of your diet. There are only twenty scientifically recommended for people over forty and eight for younger people.

3. Balance your hormonal levels. There are fourteen basic hormones, all of which must work in mutual harmony.

4. Exercise regularly, even just a thirty-minute walk a day. Exercise is vital and provides a balanced combination of aerobic activity and endurance training.

5. Fast one day a week, drinking only water between one dinner and the next. Fasting is one of the most effective therapeutic methods known to man. It is essential that those who wish to undertake longer fasts are followed by a professional therapist.

6. Do not take drugs, except temporarily antibiotics or analgesics during an emergency (of course, there are some exceptions. Diabetics, for example, must take insulin).

7. Limit or eliminate bad habits such as alcohol, coffee, recreational drugs, or sweets. You don't need to become a saint, but you must be consistent with yourself.

1. Mediterranean Breakfast Bowl

Introduction: Start your day with a burst of Mediterranean flavors with this nutritious and satisfying breakfast bowl. Packed with fresh ingredients, it's a healthy way to start the day with energy.

Prep time: 10 minutes | Cook time: 0 minutes | Yield: 2 servings

Ingredients

- 1 cup Greek yogurt
- 1/2 cup fresh berries (strawberries, blueberries or raspberries)
- 1/4 cup chopped nuts (almonds, walnuts or pistachios)
- 1/4 cup honey
- 1/2 cup granola
- 1 banana, sliced
- 1/2 cup pomegranate seeds

Method of Preparation

1. Divide the Greek yogurt between two bowls.
2. Top with fresh berries, chopped nuts, honey, granola, banana slices, and pomegranate seeds.
3. Serve immediately and enjoy!

Nutritional information (per serving): Calories: 380 | Protein: 15g | Carbohydrates: 53g | Fat: 15g | Fiber: 7g

2. Shakshuka

Introduction: Shakshuka is a classic Mediterranean breakfast dish known for its bold flavors. This spicy tomato and egg stew is perfect for sharing and will wake up your taste buds in the morning.

Prep time: 10 minutes | Cook time: 25 minutes | Yield: 4 servings

Ingredients:

- 2 tablespoons olive oil
- 1 chopped onion
- 1 red pepper, chopped
- 3 cloves garlic, minced
- 1 teaspoon ground cumin
- 1 teaspoon smoked paprika
- 1/2 teaspoon chili flakes (adjust to taste)
- 1 can (28 ounces) crushed tomatoes
- Salt and black pepper to taste
- 4-6 large eggs
- Fresh parsley, chopped, to decorate
- Feta cheese, crumbled, for garnish (optional)

Method of Preparation

1. Heat the olive oil in a large skillet over medium heat. Add the chopped onion and red pepper. Cook until softened, about 5 minutes.
2. Add the garlic, ground cumin, smoked paprika and chili flakes. Cook for 2 more minutes.
3. Pour in the crushed tomatoes and season with salt and black pepper. Simmer for 15-20 minutes or until sauce thickens.
4. Make small wells in the tomato sauce and crack the eggs into them. Cover the pan and cook until the whites are set but the yolks are still runny, about 5 to 7 minutes.
5. Garnish with chopped parsley and crumbled feta cheese if desired.
6. Serve hot with crusty bread for dipping.

Nutritional information (per serving): Calories: 220 | Protein: 10g | Carbohydrates: 16g | Fat: 14g | Fiber: 4g

3. Greek yogurt parfait

Introduction: This Greek yogurt parfait is a delicious combination of creamy yogurt, fresh fruit, and crunchy granola. It is a quick and healthy breakfast option that you will surely like.

Prep time: 5 minutes | Cook time: 0 minutes | Yield: 2 servings

Ingredients:

- 1 cup Greek yogurt
- 1/2 cup granola
- 1/2 cup of assorted red fruits (strawberries, blueberries, raspberries)
- 2 tablespoons of honey
- 1/4 cup chopped nuts (almonds, walnuts, or pecans)

Method of Preparation

1. In two serving glasses or bowls, layer Greek yogurt, granola, berries, and chopped nuts.
2. Drizzle honey on top.
3. Serve immediately or refrigerate for a healthy snack or breakfast.

Nutritional information (per serving): Calories: 320 | Protein: 14g | Carbohydrates: 36g | Fat: 14g | Fiber: 4g

4. Breakfast quesadilla with feta and spinach

Introduction: This Mediterranean-inspired breakfast quesadilla combines the rich, tangy flavor of feta cheese with the freshness of spinach and eggs. It's a perfect tasty start to your day.

Prep time: 10 minutes | Cook time: 10 minutes | Yield: 2 servings

Ingredients:

- 2 large flour tortillas
- 4 large eggs
- 1 cup of young spinach leaves
- 1/2 cup crumbled feta cheese
- Salt and black pepper to taste
- olive oil for cooking

Method of Preparation

1. In a bowl, beat the eggs and season with salt and black pepper.
2. Heat a non-stick frying pan over medium heat and add a splash of olive oil.
3. Pour the beaten eggs into the pan and stir until set.
4. Remove the scrambled eggs from the pan and set aside.
5. Place a flat tortilla in the pan. Sprinkle half the feta cheese evenly over the tortilla.
6. Add half the scrambled eggs and half the baby spinach.
7. Cover with the second tortilla and press gently.
8. Cook until tortilla is golden brown and crispy, about 2-3 minutes per side.
9. Remove from heat and let cool for a minute before cutting into wedges.
10. Serve hot.

Nutritional information (per serving): Calories: 400 | Protein: 18g | Carbohydrates: 25g | Fat: 25g | Fiber: 2g

5. Breakfast Frittata with Olives and Tomato

Introduction: This Mediterranean frittata is a colorful and tasty dish, perfect for breakfast or brunch. It's loaded with olives, tomatoes, and herbs to give it a burst of Mediterranean flavor.

Prep time: 10 minutes | Cook time: 20 minutes | Yield: 4 servings

Ingredients:

- 8 large eggs
- 1/2 cup chopped Kalamata olives
- 1 cup cherry tomatoes, cut in half
- 1/2 cup crumbled feta cheese
- 2 tablespoons fresh basil, chopped
- 2 tablespoons fresh parsley, chopped
- Salt and black pepper to taste
- olive oil for cooking

Method of Preparation

1. Preheat oven to 375°F (190°C).
2. In a bowl, beat the eggs and season with salt and black pepper.
3. Heat an oven-safe frying pan over medium heat and add a splash of olive oil.
4. Add the olives and cherry tomatoes to the pan and cook for 2-3 minutes.
5. Pour the beaten eggs evenly over the olives and tomatoes.
6. Sprinkle with crumbled feta cheese, chopped basil and chopped parsley.
7. Cook for 3-4 minutes on the stove until the edges set.
8. Transfer the pan to the preheated oven and bake for 12 to 15 minutes, or until the frittata is puffed and set in the center.
9. Remove from the oven and let cool for a few minutes before cutting.
10. Serve warm or at room temperature.

Nutritional information (per serving): Calories: 240 | Protein: 15g | Carbohydrates: 5g | Fat: 17g | Fiber: 2g

6. Turkish Menemen

Introduction: Menemen is a popular Turkish breakfast dish that includes eggs, tomatoes and spices. It's a quick and tasty way to start the day with the taste of Turkey.

Prep time: 10 minutes | Cook time: 15 minutes | Yield: 2 servings

Ingredients:

- 2 tablespoons olive oil
- 1 chopped onion
- 1 red pepper, chopped
- 2 cloves garlic, minced
- 2 tomatoes, chopped
- 1 teaspoon ground cumin
- 1/2 teaspoon paprika
- 4 large eggs
- Salt and black pepper to taste
- Fresh parsley, chopped, to decorate

Method of Preparation

1. Heat the olive oil in a large skillet over medium heat.
2. Add the chopped onion and red pepper. Cook until softened, about 5 minutes.
3. Add the minced garlic and cook for 2 more minutes.
4. Add the chopped tomatoes, ground cumin and paprika. Cook for 5-7 minutes until the tomatoes break down and the mixture thickens.
5. Make small wells in the tomato mixture and crack the eggs into them.
6. Season the eggs with salt and black pepper.
7. Cover the pan and cook until the whites are set but the yolks are still runny, about 5 to 7 minutes.
8. Garnish with fresh chopped parsley.
9. Serve hot with crusty bread.

Nutritional information (per serving): Calories: 230 | Protein: 9g | Carbohydrates: 14g | Fat: 17g | Fiber: 4g

7. Mediterranean Avocado Toast

Introduction: Avocado toast gets a Mediterranean touch with this recipe. Creamy avocado, juicy tomatoes, and tangy feta cheese combine on crisp toast for a simple but satisfying breakfast.

Prep time: 10 minutes | Cook time: 5 minutes | Yield: 2 servings

Ingredients:

- 2 slices of whole wheat bread, toasted
- 1 ripe avocado, mashed
- 1 cup cherry tomatoes, cut in half
- 1/2 cup crumbled feta cheese
- Fresh basil leaves, to decorate.
- Balsamic glaze, for drizzling (optional)
- Salt and black pepper to taste

Method of Preparation

1. Toast the bread slices until crispy.
2. Spread mashed avocado evenly over toast.
3. Top with cherry tomato halves and crumbled feta cheese.
4. Garnish with fresh basil leaves.
5. Drizzle with balsamic glaze if desired.
6. Season with salt and black pepper.
7. Serve immediately.

Nutritional information (per serving): Calories: 320 | Protein: 10g | Carbohydrates: 28g | Fat: 21g | Fiber: 9g

8. Mediterranean Omelet

Introduction: This Mediterranean-inspired omelette is a breakfast option packed with protein, colorful vegetables, and savory flavors. It's a satisfying and nutritious way to start the day.

Prep time: 10 minutes | Cook time: 10 minutes | Yield: 2 servings

Ingredients:

- 4 large eggs
- 1/4 cup red pepper, diced
- 1/4 cup red onion, chopped
- 1/4 cup cherry tomatoes, cut in half
- 1/4 cup baby spinach leaves
- 1/4 cup feta cheese, crumbled
- 2 tablespoons fresh parsley, chopped
- Salt and black pepper to taste
- olive oil for cooking

Method of Preparation

1. In a bowl, beat the eggs and season with salt and black pepper.
2. Heat a non-stick frying pan over medium heat and add a splash of olive oil.
3. Add the chopped red pepper and red onion. Cook until softened, about 3 to 4 minutes.
4. Pour the beaten eggs into the pan.
5. Add the cherry tomatoes, baby spinach, and crumbled feta cheese evenly over the eggs.
6. Cook until the edges of the tortilla begin to set, about 3 to 4 minutes.
7. Carefully fold the tortilla in half with a spatula and cook for a further 2-3 minutes until the center is set.
8. Sprinkle with fresh chopped parsley.
9. Serve hot.

Nutritional information (per serving): Calories: 260 | Protein: 16g | Carbohydrates: 6g | Fat: 19g | Fiber: 2g

9. Labneh with Honey and Pistachios

Introduction: Labneh is a strained creamy yogurt cheese popular in Mediterranean cuisine. When drizzled with honey and sprinkled with pistachios, it makes a delicious and healthy breakfast.

Prep time: 5 minutes (plus straining time) | Cook time: 0 minutes | Yield: 2 servings

Ingredients:

- 1 cup Greek yogurt
- 2 tablespoons of honey
- 2 tablespoons chopped pistachios

Method of Preparation

1. Place a fine-mesh strainer over a bowl and cover it with cheesecloth or a clean kitchen towel.
2. Pour the Greek yogurt into the strainer.
3. Cover and refrigerate for at least 2 hours or overnight to allow excess liquid to drain.
4. Once strained, transfer the labneh to serving bowls.
5. Drizzle honey over the labneh.
6. Sprinkle with chopped pistachios.
7. Serve with pita bread, fresh fruit or toast.

Nutritional information (per serving): Calories: 160 | Protein: 7g | Carbohydrates: 16g | Fat: 8g | Fiber: 1g

10. Mediterranean Breakfast Burrito

Introduction: This breakfast burrito brings together Mediterranean flavors in a convenient wrapper. It's packed with eggs, veggies, and feta cheese for a delicious, portable breakfast.

Preparation time: 15 minutes | Cooking time: 10 minutes | Yield: 2 servings

Ingredients

- 4 large eggs
- 1/4 cup red pepper, diced
- 1/4 cup red onion, chopped
- 1/4 cup cherry tomatoes, cut in half
- 1/4 cup crumbled feta cheese
- 2 tablespoons fresh parsley, chopped
- Salt and black pepper to taste
- 2 large whole wheat tortillas
- olive oil for cooking

Method of Preparation

1. In a bowl, beat the eggs and season with salt and black pepper.
2. Heat a non-stick frying pan over medium heat and add a splash of olive oil.
3. Add the chopped red pepper and red onion. Cook until softened, about 3 to 4 minutes.
4. Pour the beaten eggs into the pan.
5. Add the cherry tomatoes and crumbled feta cheese evenly over the eggs.
6. Cook until the eggs are scrambled and set, about 3 to 4 minutes.
7. Sprinkle with fresh chopped parsley.
8. Heat the tortillas in a dry skillet or in the microwave.
9. Pour the scrambled egg mixture over the tortillas.
10. Roll the tortillas into burritos and serve immediately.

Nutritional information (per serving): Calories: 340 | Protein: 15g | Carbohydrates: 26g | Fat: 20g | Fiber: 4g

11. Mediterranean scrambled eggs

Introduction: These Mediterranean-style scrambled eggs are a quick and tasty way to start the day. With the addition of olives, tomatoes and herbs, they are a savory delight.

Prep time: 10 minutes | Cook time: 5 minutes | Yield: 2 servings

Ingredients:

- 4 large eggs
- 1/4 cup chopped Kalamata olives
- 1/4 cup cherry tomatoes, cut in half
- 2 tablespoons chopped fresh parsley
- Salt and black pepper to taste
- olive oil for cooking

Method of Preparation

1. In a bowl, beat the eggs and season with salt and black pepper.
2. Heat a non-stick frying pan over medium heat and add a splash of olive oil.
3. Add the chopped Kalamata olives and cherry tomatoes to the pan. Cook for 2-3 minutes.
4. Pour the beaten eggs into the skillet and cook, stirring gently, until the eggs are scrambled and set, about 2 to 3 minutes.
5. Sprinkle with fresh chopped parsley.
6. Serve hot.

Nutritional information (per serving): Calories: 180 | Protein: 11g | Carbohydrates: 4g | Fat: 14g | Fiber: 1g

12. Quinoa for Mediterranean breakfast

Introduction: This Mediterranean quinoa breakfast is a healthy and nutritious breakfast. It's packed with protein and fiber to keep you satisfied all day long.

Preparation time: 10 minutes | Cooking time: 15 minutes | Yield: 2 servings

Ingredients:

- 1/2 cup quinoa, rinsed and drained
- 1 cup of water
- 1/4 cup diced cucumber
- 1/4 cup diced tomato
- 1/4 cup chopped fresh parsley
- 2 tablespoons chopped Kalamata olives
- 2 tablespoons crumbled feta cheese
- 2 tablespoons extra virgin olive oil
- 1 tablespoon lemon juice
- Salt and black pepper to taste

Method of Preparation

1. In a small saucepan, bring water to a boil. Add quinoa, reduce heat to low, cover and simmer for 12 to 15 minutes or until quinoa is tender and water is absorbed.
2. Fluff the cooked quinoa with a fork and let it cool for a few minutes.
3. In a large bowl, combine the cooked quinoa, diced cucumber, diced tomato, chopped fresh parsley, and chopped Kalamata olives.
4. In a small bowl, whisk together the extra virgin olive oil and lemon juice. Season with salt and black pepper.
5. Drizzle dressing over quinoa mixture and toss to combine.
6. Sprinkle with crumbled feta cheese.

7. Serve warm or at room temperature.

Nutritional information (per serving): Calories: 300 | Protein: 7g | Carbohydrates: 26g | Fat: 19g | Fiber: 4g

13. Spanakopita Breakfast Casserole

Introduction: This Spanakopita-inspired breakfast casserole is a Greek delight. It's a tasty mix of spinach, feta cheese and eggs baked to perfection.

Prep time: 20 minutes | Cook time: 40 minutes | Yield: 6 servings

Ingredients:

- 1 package (10 ounces) frozen chopped spinach, thawed and drained
- 1/2 cup crumbled feta cheese
- 1/2 cup grated Parmesan cheese
- 1/2 cup chopped fresh dill
- 4 large eggs
- 1/2 cup of milk
- Salt and black pepper to taste
- Olive oil to grease the baking dish.

Method of Preparation

1. Preheat oven to 375°F (190°C). Grease a baking dish with olive oil.
2. In a large bowl, combine the thawed and drained chopped spinach, crumbled feta cheese, grated Parmesan cheese, and chopped fresh dill.
3. In another bowl, whisk together the eggs, milk, salt and black pepper.
4. Pour egg mixture over spinach and cheese mixture. Stir to combine.
5. Transfer the mixture to the greased baking dish.

6. Bake for 35-40 minutes, or until the top is golden brown and the casserole is ready.
7. Let it cool for a few minutes before cutting and serving.

Nutritional information (per serving):
Calories: 170 | Protein: 11g | Carbohydrates: 5g | Fat: 12g

Fiber: 2g

4. Drizzle honey over each bowl.
5. Top with chopped mixed nuts and fresh berries.
6. Add a tablespoon of Greek yogurt on top.
7. Serve hot.

Nutritional information (per serving):
Calories: 390 | Protein: 14g | Carbohydrates: 55g | Fat: 15g | Fiber: 6g

14. Greek oatmeal with honey and walnuts

Introduction: This Greek-inspired oatmeal is a comforting and nutritious breakfast option. Combine hearty oats with the sweetness of honey and the crunch of nuts for a delicious breakfast.

Prep time: 5 minutes | Cook time: 10 minutes | Yield: 2 servings

Ingredients:

- 1 cup oat flakes
- 2 cups of milk (dairy or vegetable)
- 2 tablespoons of honey
- 1/4 cup chopped mixed nuts (walnuts, almonds, or pecans)
- 1/4 cup fresh berries (strawberries, blueberries or raspberries)
- 2 tablespoons Greek yogurt

Preparation method:

1. In a saucepan, bring milk to a boil over medium heat.
2. Add the rolled oats and reduce the heat to low. Cook, stirring occasionally, for 5 to 7 minutes or until oats are tender and mixture thickens.
3. Divide the cooked oats between two serving bowls.

15. Mediterranean Breakfast Wrap

Introduction: This Mediterranean breakfast wrap is a convenient and satisfying breakfast that you can enjoy on the go. It is full of flavors and nutrients.

Preparation time: 10 minutes | Cooking time: 5 minutes | Yield: 2 servings

Ingredients:

- 2 large whole wheat tortillas
- 4 large eggs
- 1/4 cup chopped red pepper
- 1/4 cup chopped red onion
- 1/4 cup crumbled feta cheese
- 2 tablespoons fresh parsley, chopped
- Salt and black pepper to taste
- olive oil for cooking

Method of Preparation

1. In a bowl, beat the eggs and season with salt and black pepper.
2. Heat a non-stick frying pan over medium heat and add a splash of olive oil.
3. Add the chopped red pepper and red onion. Cook until softened, about 3 to 4 minutes.
4. Pour the beaten eggs into the pan.

5. Add the crumbled feta cheese evenly over the eggs.
6. Cook, stirring gently, until the eggs are scrambled and set, about 2 to 3 minutes.
7. Sprinkle with fresh chopped parsley.
8. Heat the tortillas in a dry skillet or in the microwave.
9. Pour the scrambled egg mixture over the tortillas.
10. Roll up the tortillas and serve immediately.

Nutritional information (per serving):
Calories: 330 | Protein: 17g | Carbohydrates: 21g | Fat: 20g | Fiber: 3g

MEDITERRANEAN SIDE DISH

1. Tzatziki Sauce

Introduction: Tzatziki sauce is a creamy, refreshing Greek condiment made with yogurt, cucumber, and fresh herbs. It is a perfect sauce or sauce for Mediterranean dishes.

Prep time: 10 minutes | Cook time: 0 minutes | Yield: approximately 2 cups

Ingredients:

- 1 cucumber, peeled, seeded and grated
- 2 cups of Greek yogurt
- 2 cloves garlic, minced
- 1 tablespoon fresh dill, chopped
- 1 tablespoon fresh mint, chopped
- 1 tablespoon extra virgin olive oil
- 1 tablespoon lemon juice
- Salt and black pepper to taste

Method of Preparation

1. Grate the cucumber and squeeze out excess moisture with a clean kitchen towel.
2. In a bowl, combine the grated cucumber, Greek yogurt, minced garlic, minced dill, minced mint, olive oil, and lemon juice.
3. Mix well until all ingredients are well combined.
4. Season with salt and black pepper to taste.
5. Refrigerate for at least 30 minutes to allow the flavors to blend.
6. Serve cold.

Nutritional information (per 2 tablespoon serving): Calories: 25 | Protein: 2g | Carbohydrates: 2g | Fat: 1g | Fiber: 0g

2. Greek Salad

Introduction: Greek salad, also known as Horiatiki salad, is a classic Mediterranean salad full of freshness. It's a combination of crunchy vegetables, feta cheese, olives and a spicy dressing.

Prep time: 15 minutes | Cook time: 0 minutes | Yield: 4 servings

Ingredients:

- 2 large tomatoes, diced
- 1 cucumber, diced
- 1 red onion, thinly sliced
- 1 green pepper, diced
- 1/2 cup Kalamata olives, pitted
- 1/2 cup crumbled feta cheese
- 2 tablespoons extra virgin olive oil
- 1 tablespoon red wine vinegar
- 1 teaspoon dried oregano
- Salt and black pepper to taste
- Fresh parsley, to decorate

Method of Preparation

1. In a large salad bowl, combine the diced tomatoes, diced cucumber, thinly sliced red onion, diced green pepper, and Kalamata olives.
2. Sprinkle crumbled feta cheese on top.
3. In a small bowl, whisk together the extra virgin olive oil, red wine vinegar, dried oregano, salt, and black pepper.
4. Drizzle dressing over salad and toss to combine.
5. Garnish with fresh parsley.
6. Serve immediately.

Nutritional information (per serving): Calories: 180 | Protein: 4g | Carbohydrates: 10g | Fat: 14g | Fiber: 3g

3. Roasted Mediterranean vegetables

Introduction: Roasted Mediterranean vegetables are a tasty and colorful side dish. It's a simple way to enjoy the natural sweetness of vegetables with Mediterranean herbs and olive oil.

Prep time: 10 minutes | Cook time: 30 minutes | Yield: 4 servings

Ingredients:

- 2 cups cherry tomatoes
- 1 red pepper, cut into strips
- 1 yellow bell pepper, cut into strips
- 1 zucchini, sliced
- 1 red onion, cut into wedges
- 1/4 cup extra virgin olive oil
- 2 cloves garlic, minced
- 1 teaspoon dried oregano
- Salt and black pepper to taste
- Fresh basil leaves, to decorate.

Method of Preparation

1. Preheat oven to 425°F (220°C).
2. In a large bowl, combine cherry tomatoes, red bell pepper, yellow bell pepper, zucchini, and red onion.
3. In a separate bowl, whisk together the extra virgin olive oil, minced garlic, dried oregano, salt, and black pepper.
4. Drizzle olive oil mixture over vegetables and toss to coat.
5. Spread vegetables in a single layer on a baking sheet.
6. Roast in the preheated oven for 25-30 minutes, or until the vegetables are tender and lightly caramelized.
7. Garnish with fresh basil leaves.

8. Serve hot or at room temperature.

Nutritional information (per serving): Calories: 180 | Protein: 2g | Carbohydrates: 12g | Fat: 14g | Fiber: 3g

4. Humus

Introduction: Hummus is a creamy dip made with chickpeas, tahini, garlic, and lemon juice. It is a versatile side dish or appetizer that is popular throughout the Mediterranean region.

Prep time: 10 minutes | Cook time: 0 minutes | Yield: approximately 2 cups

Ingredients:

- 1 can (15 ounces) chickpeas, drained and rinsed
- 1/4 cup tahini
- 2 cloves garlic, minced
- 3 tablespoons lemon juice
- 2 tablespoons extra virgin olive oil
- 1/2 teaspoon ground cumin
- Salt and black pepper to taste
- Paprika and olive oil, to decorate (optional)

Preparation method:

1. In a food processor, combine the chickpeas, tahini, minced garlic, lemon juice, extra virgin olive oil, ground cumin, salt and black pepper.
2. Process until smooth and creamy, adding a little water if necessary to reach desired consistency.
3. Taste and adjust seasoning as needed.
4. Transfer hummus to a serving bowl.
5. If you wish, decorate with a pinch of paprika and a drizzle of olive oil.

6. Serve with pita bread, vegetables or as a sauce.

Nutritional information (per 2 tablespoon serving): Calories: 45 | Protein: 2g | Carbohydrates: 4g | Fat: 3g | Fiber: 1g

5. Tabuli Salad

Introduction: Tabouli, also known as tabbouleh, is a refreshing and vibrant salad made with bulgur wheat, fresh herbs and vegetables. It is a staple of Mediterranean and Middle Eastern cuisines.

Prep time: 15 minutes | Cooking time: 0 minutes | Yield: 4 servings

Ingredients:

- 1 cup bulgur wheat
- 1 1/2 cups boiling water
- 2 cups fresh parsley, finely chopped
- 1/2 cup fresh mint leaves, finely chopped
- 2 tomatoes, diced
- 1 cucumber, diced
- 1/4 cup red onion, finely chopped
- 1/4 cup extra virgin olive oil
- 1/4 cup lemon juice
- Salt and black pepper to taste
- Optional: romaine lettuce leaves to serve

Method of Preparation

1. Place the bulgur wheat in a heatproof bowl. Pour boiling water over it, cover and let sit for 15 minutes or until water is absorbed.
2. Stir the cooked bulgur with a fork and let it cool.
3. In a large salad bowl, combine the finely chopped fresh parsley and mint.

4. Add the diced tomatoes, diced cucumber, and finely chopped red onion to the bowl.
5. In a small bowl, whisk together the extra virgin olive oil, lemon juice, salt, and black pepper.
6. Pour the dressing over the salad and toss to combine.
7. Serve tabouli salad on romaine lettuce leaves, if desired.

Nutritional information (per serving): Calories: 230 | Protein: 4g | Carbohydrates: 28g | Fat: 12g | Fiber: 6g

6. Stuffed grape leaves (Dolmas)

Introduction: Stuffed grape leaves, known as dolmas, are a Mediterranean delicacy. These tender grape leaves are stuffed with a tasty blend of rice, herbs and spices.

Prep time: 30 minutes | Cook time: 45 minutes | Yield: Approximately 24 stuffed grape leaves.

Ingredients:

- 1 jar (8 ounces) brined grape leaves, drained and rinsed
- 1 cup long grain white rice
- 1/2 cup extra virgin olive oil
- 1/4 cup fresh lemon juice
- 1/4 cup fresh dill, chopped
- 1/4 cup fresh mint, chopped
- 1/4 cup fresh parsley, chopped
- 1 small onion, finely chopped
- 2 cloves garlic, minced
- Salt and black pepper to taste
- Lemon slices, to decorate

Method of Preparation

1. Rinse the grape leaves thoroughly under cold running water. Drain and reserve.
2. In a large bowl, combine long grain white rice, extra virgin olive oil, fresh lemon juice, chopped fresh dill, chopped fresh mint, chopped fresh parsley, finely chopped onion, minced garlic, salt and black pepper. Mix well.
3. Take a grape leaf and place it shiny side down on a clean work surface.
4. Trim tough stems if necessary.
5. Place about 1 tablespoon of the rice mixture in the center of the sheet.
6. Fold the sides of the leaf over the filling and then roll it tightly into a small cylinder.
7. Repeat with remaining grape leaves and filling.
8. Place the stuffed grape leaves in a large pot, seam side down, in a single layer.
9. Pour enough water over the stuffed grape leaves to cover them.
10. Place a heatproof plate or a few lemon slices on top of the grape leaves to make them heavier.
11. Cover the pot and simmer for 45 minutes, or until the rice is cooked and the grape leaves are tender.
12. Let the dolmas cool to room temperature before serving.

Nutritional information (per serving of 2 dolmas): Calories: 180 | Protein: 2g | Carbohydrates: 18g | Fat: 11g | Fiber: 1g

7. Mediterranean rice pilaf

Introduction: Mediterranean rice pilaf is a tasty and aromatic side dish made with rice, vegetables and aromatic spices. It is a wonderful accompaniment to many Mediterranean dishes.

Preparation time: 10 minutes | Cooking time: 25 minutes | Yield: 4 servings

Ingredients:

- 1 cup long grain white rice
- 2 cups of vegetable broth
- 1/4 cup chopped red pepper
- 1/4 cup diced green bell pepper
- 1/4 cup chopped red onion
- 1/4 cup diced zucchini
- 1/4 cup chopped carrot
- 2 cloves garlic, minced
- 2 tablespoons extra virgin olive oil
- 1/2 teaspoon ground cumin
- 1/2 teaspoon ground cilantro
- Salt and black pepper to taste
- Fresh parsley, to decorate

Method of Preparation

1. In a large skillet, heat the extra virgin olive oil over medium heat.
2. Add minced garlic and sauté for 1-2 minutes until fragrant.
3. Add the chopped red pepper, chopped green pepper, chopped red onion, chopped zucchini, and chopped carrot. Sauté for 5 minutes or until vegetables begin to soften.
4. Add long grain white rice, ground cumin, and ground cilantro. Cook, stirring constantly, for a further 2-3 minutes until the rice is lightly toasted.
5. Pour in the vegetable broth and bring to a boil.
6. Reduce heat to low, cover, and simmer for 15 to 20 minutes, or until rice is tender and liquid is absorbed.
7. Season with salt and black pepper to taste.
8. Garnish with fresh parsley.
9. Stir the rice with a fork before serving.

Nutritional information (per serving): Calories: 260 | Protein: 4g | Carbohydrates: 44g | Fat: 7g | Fiber: 2g

8. Baba Ganush

Introduction: Baba Ganoush is a creamy, smoky eggplant sauce that is a favorite in Mediterranean cuisine. It is made with roasted eggplant, tahini, garlic and lemon juice.

Prep time: 15 minutes | Cook time: 30 minutes | Yield: approximately 2 cups

Ingredients:

- 2 large eggplants
- 2 cloves garlic, minced
- 1/4 cup tahini
- 2 tablespoons extra virgin olive oil
- 2 tablespoons lemon juice
- 1/2 teaspoon ground cumin
- Salt and black pepper to taste
- Fresh parsley and a splash of olive oil, to decorate

Method of Preparation

1. Preheat the oven to 400°F (200°C).
2. Prick the eggplants with a fork and place them on a baking sheet.
3. Roast the eggplants in the preheated oven for 25 to 30 minutes, or until the skin is charred and the flesh is soft.
4. Take the eggplants out of the oven and let them cool slightly.
5. Peel the eggplants and discard the skin.
6. Place the peeled eggplant pulp in a food processor.
7. Add the minced garlic, tahini, extra virgin olive oil, lemon juice, ground cumin, salt and black pepper.
8. Process until smooth and creamy.

9. Taste and adjust seasoning as needed.
10. Transfer the baba ganoush to a serving bowl.
11. Garnish with fresh parsley and a drizzle of olive oil.
12. Serve with pita bread or vegetables for dipping.

Nutritional information (per 2 tablespoon serving): Calories: 30 | Protein: 1g | Carbohydrates: 3g | Fat: 2g | Fiber: 1g

9. Greek roast potatoes

Introduction: Greek roast potatoes are a tasty and flavorful side dish that pairs well with several Mediterranean main dishes. They are seasoned with herbs and roasted to perfection.

Prep time: 15 minutes | Cook time: 45 minutes | Yield: 4 servings

Ingredients:

- 4 large russet potatoes, peeled and cut into wedges
- 1/4 cup extra virgin olive oil
- 2 cloves garlic, minced
- 1 teaspoon dried oregano
- 1 teaspoon dried thyme
- Salt and black pepper to taste
- Fresh parsley, to decorate
- Lemon wedges, to serve (optional)

Method of Preparation

1. Preheat oven to 425°F (220°C).
2. In a large bowl, combine the potato slices, minced garlic, extra virgin olive oil, dried oregano, dried thyme, salt, and black pepper.

3. Toss the potatoes until they are evenly coated with the seasoning mixture.
4. Spread the seasoned potato slices in a single layer on a baking sheet.
5. Roast in the preheated oven for 40-45 minutes, or until the potatoes are golden brown and crispy on the outside and tender on the inside.
6. Garnish with fresh parsley and serve hot.
7. Optionally, serve with lemon wedges to squeeze over the potatoes.

Nutritional information (per serving): Calories: 280 | Protein: 4g | Carbohydrates: 40g | Fat: 12g | Fiber: 3g

10. Fat salad

Introduction: Fattoush is a refreshing and spicy Lebanese salad featuring crispy pita bread, fresh vegetables and a spicy dressing. It is a delicious garnish.

Prep time: 15 minutes | Cook time: 5 minute | Yield: 4 servings

Ingredients:

- 2 cups diced cucumber
- 2 cups diced tomato
- 1 cup chopped red pepper
- 1 cup diced green bell pepper
- 1/2 cup chopped red onion
- 1/4 cup chopped fresh parsley
- 1/4 cup chopped fresh mint
- 2 small slices of pita bread, toasted and broken into pieces
- 1/4 cup extra virgin olive oil
- 2 tablespoons fresh lemon juice
- 1 teaspoon ground sumac (optional)
- Salt and black pepper to taste

Method of Preparation

1. In a large salad bowl, combine the diced cucumber, diced tomato, diced red pepper, diced green pepper, diced red onion, chopped fresh parsley, and chopped fresh mint.
2. Add the toasted and broken pita bread pieces to the bowl.
3. In a small bowl, whisk together the extra virgin olive oil, fresh lemon juice, ground sumac (if using), salt, and black pepper.
4. Drizzle dressing over salad and toss to combine.
5. Serve immediately to enjoy the crispy pita before it softens.

Nutritional information (per serving): Calories: 250 | Protein: 4g | Carbohydrates: 29g | Fat: 14g | Fiber: 5g

11. Mediterranean couscous salad

Introduction: Mediterranean Couscous Salad is a light and flavorful side dish that includes couscous, colorful vegetables, and a tasty lemon-herb dressing.

Prep time: 15 minutes | Cook time: 5 minutes | Yield: 4 servings

Ingredients:

- 1 cup couscous
- 1 1/4 cups vegetable broth
- 1 cup diced cucumber
- 1 cup diced tomato
- 1/2 cup chopped red onion
- 1/4 cup chopped fresh parsley
- 1/4 cup chopped fresh mint
- 2 tablespoons extra virgin olive oil
- 2 tablespoons fresh lemon juice
- 1 teaspoon lemon zest

- Salt and black pepper to taste

Method of Preparation

1. In a saucepan, bring the vegetable broth to a boil.
2. Add the couscous, remove from heat and cover. Let it sit for 5 minutes.
3. Stir the cooked couscous with a fork and let it cool.
4. In a large salad bowl, combine the cooked couscous, diced cucumber, diced tomato, diced red onion, chopped fresh parsley, and chopped fresh mint.
5. In a small bowl, whisk together the extra virgin olive oil, fresh lemon juice, lemon zest, salt, and black pepper.
6. Drizzle dressing over salad and toss to combine.
7. Serve at room temperature or cold.

Nutritional information (per serving): Calories: 260 | Protein: 6g | Carbohydrates: 44g | Fat: 7g | Fiber: 4g

12. Spanakopita (spinach pie)

Introduction: Spanakopita is a classic Greek dish made with layers of puff filo pastry filled with a savory mix of spinach, feta cheese, and herbs.

Prep time: 30 minutes | Cook time: 45 minutes | Yield: 8 servings

Ingredients:

- 1 package (16 ounces) frozen chopped spinach, thawed and drained
- 1 cup crumbled feta cheese
- 1/2 cup grated Parmesan cheese
- 1/2 cup chopped fresh dill
- 4 green onions, chopped
- 2 cloves garlic, minced

- 4 large eggs, lightly beaten
- 1/4 cup extra virgin olive oil
- 16 sheets of filo dough, thawed
- Cooking spray or melted butter for brushing
- Salt and black pepper to taste

Method of Preparation

1. Preheat oven to 350°F (175°C).
2. In a large bowl, combine the thawed and drained chopped spinach, crumbled feta cheese, grated Parmesan cheese, chopped fresh dill, chopped green onions, minced garlic, and lightly beaten eggs.
3. Mix well and season with salt and black pepper to taste.
4. Coat a 9x13-inch baking dish with melted butter or cooking spray.
5. Place one sheet of phyllo dough on the plate and brush with melted butter or cooking spray.
6. Repeat with 7 more sheets of phyllo dough, layering and brushing each sheet with butter or cooking spray.
7. Spread the spinach and cheese mixture over the phyllo dough layers.
8. Place the remaining 8 sheets of phyllo dough on top, brushing each sheet with butter or cooking spray.
9. Using a sharp knife, cut the top layer of phyllo dough into serving-sized pieces.
10. Bake in the preheated oven for 45 minutes, or until the spanakopita is golden brown and set.
11. Let it cool for a few minutes before serving.

Nutritional information (per serving):
Calories: 280 | Protein: 9g | Carbohydrates: 20g | Fat: 19g | Fiber: 2g

13. Falafel

Introduction: Falafel is a much-loved Middle Eastern dish made with ground chickpeas or fava beans, flavored with herbs and spices and fried to crispy perfection. They can be served as a side dish or in a pita sandwich.

Prep time: 20 minutes | Cook time: 15 minutes (per batch) | Yield: approximately 24 falafel

Ingredients:

- 2 cups cooked chickpeas (or 1 can, drained and rinsed)
- 1/2 cup fresh parsley, chopped
- 1/2 cup fresh cilantro, chopped
- 1/2 cup chopped onion
- 3 cloves garlic, minced
- 1 teaspoon ground cumin
- 1 teaspoon ground coriander
- 1/4 teaspoon cayenne pepper (optional, for spiciness)
- Salt and black pepper to taste
- 2 tablespoons all-purpose flour
- 1 teaspoon baking powder
- Vegetable oil for frying

Method of Preparation

1. In a food processor, combine the cooked chickpeas, fresh parsley, fresh cilantro, chopped onion, minced garlic, ground cumin, ground coriander, cayenne pepper (if using), salt, and pepper. black.
2. Pulse the mixture until a thick paste forms. Be careful not to process too much; You want a slightly textured mix.
3. Transfer the mixture to a bowl and add the all-purpose flour and baking powder.
4. Form the mixture into golf ball-sized balls and flatten them slightly to create patties.
5. Heat the vegetable oil in a deep skillet or skillet over medium-high heat.
6. Fry the falafel in batches until golden brown and crispy, about 2-3 minutes per side.

7. Remove falafel from oil and drain on paper towels.
8. Serve hot with pita bread, tahini sauce and fresh vegetables.

Nutritional information (per falafel): Calories: 50 | Protein: 2g | Carbohydrates: 8g | Fat: 1g | Fiber: 2g

14. Mediterranean chickpea salad

Introduction: Mediterranean chickpea salad is a refreshing and protein-rich side dish. Contains chickpeas, fresh vegetables and Mediterranean flavors.

Prep time: 15 minutes | Cook time: 0 minutes | Yield: 4 servings

Ingredients:

- 2 cans (15 ounces each) chickpeas, drained and rinsed
- 1 cup diced cucumber
- 1 cup diced tomato
- 1/2 cup chopped red onion
- 1/4 cup chopped fresh parsley
- 1/4 cup chopped fresh mint
- 1/4 cup extra virgin olive oil
- 2 tablespoons fresh lemon juice
- 1 teaspoon ground cumin
- Salt and black pepper to taste
- Crumbled feta cheese (optional)

Method of Preparation

1. In a large salad bowl, combine the drained and rinsed chickpeas, diced cucumber, diced tomato, diced red onion, chopped fresh parsley, and chopped fresh mint.

2. In a small bowl, whisk together the extra virgin olive oil, fresh lemon juice, ground cumin, salt, and black pepper.
3. Drizzle dressing over salad and toss to combine.
4. If desired, sprinkle with crumbled feta cheese.
5. Serve cold or at room temperature.

Nutritional information (per serving): Calories: 320 | Protein: 10g | Carbohydrates: 32g | Fat: 18g | Fiber: 9g

15. Marinated Olives

Introduction: Marinated olives are a simple but tasty side dish or appetizer. They are marinated in a mixture of olive oil and Mediterranean herbs and spices.

Prep time: 10 minutes | Cook time: 0 minutes | Yield: 4 servings

Ingredients:

- 2 cups mixed Mediterranean olives (green and black)
- 1/4 cup extra virgin olive oil
- 2 cloves garlic, minced
- 1 teaspoon dried oregano
- 1/2 teaspoon red pepper flakes (adjust to taste)
- Zest of 1 lemon
- Sprigs of fresh thyme (optional, to decorate)

Method of Preparation

1. In a bowl, combine the Mediterranean olive mixture.
2. In a separate bowl, whisk together the extra virgin olive oil, minced garlic, dried oregano, red pepper flakes, and lemon zest.
3. Pour the olive oil mixture over the olives and toss to coat.

4. Let the olives marinate at room temperature for at least 30 minutes before serving.
5. If desired, garnish with fresh thyme sprigs.
6. Serve as a garnish or appetizer.

Nutritional information (per serving): Calories: 180 | Protein: 0g | Carbohydrates: 3g | Fat: 18g | Fiber: 2g

MEDITERRANEAN PASTA, GRAINS AND BEANS

1. Mediterranean Quinoa Salad

Introduction: Mediterranean Quinoa Salad is a light and nutritious dish that contains quinoa, fresh vegetables and Mediterranean flavors. It is perfect for a healthy side or main dish.

Prep time: 15 minutes | Cook time: 15 minutes | Yield: 4 servings

Ingredients:

- 1 cup quinoa, rinsed
- 2 cups of water or vegetable broth
- 1 cup cherry tomatoes, cut in half
- 1 cucumber, diced
- 1/2 cup Kalamata olives, pitted and sliced
- 1/2 cup crumbled feta cheese
- 1/4 cup red onion, finely chopped
- 2 tablespoons fresh parsley, chopped
- 2 tablespoons fresh mint, chopped
- 1/4 cup extra virgin olive oil
- 2 tablespoons fresh lemon juice
- Salt and black pepper to taste

Method of Preparation

1. In a saucepan, combine the quinoa and water or vegetable broth. Bring to a boil, then reduce heat to low, cover and simmer for 15 minutes or until quinoa is cooked and liquid is absorbed. Remove from heat and let cool.
2. In a large bowl, combine the cooked quinoa, cherry tomatoes, diced cucumber, Kalamata olives, crumbled feta cheese, finely chopped red onion, chopped fresh parsley, and chopped fresh mint.
3. In a small bowl, whisk together the extra virgin olive oil, fresh lemon juice, salt, and black pepper.

4. Drizzle dressing over salad and toss to combine.
5. Serve cold.

Nutritional information (per serving):
Calories: 350 | Protein: 9g | Carbohydrates: 37g | Fat: 20g | Fiber: 5g

2. Greek lentil soup

Introduction: Greek lentil soup, known as "fakes," is a hearty, comforting dish made with lentils, vegetables, and Mediterranean spices. It is a staple in Greek cuisine.

Prep time: 15 minutes | Cooking time: 45 minutes | Yield: 6 servings

Ingredients:

- 1 cup brown or green lentils, rinsed and drained
- 1 chopped onion
- 2 carrots, diced
- 2 stalks celery, diced
- 3 cloves garlic, minced
- 2 tablespoons extra virgin olive oil
- 1 can (14.5 ounces) diced tomatoes
- 1 teaspoon dried oregano
- 1 teaspoon dried thyme
- 6 cups of vegetable broth
- Salt and black pepper to taste
- Fresh parsley, to decorate
- Red wine vinegar (optional, to serve)

Method of Preparation

1. In a large pot, heat the extra virgin olive oil over medium heat.
2. Add chopped onion, chopped carrots and chopped celery. Sauté for 5-7 minutes until the vegetables begin to soften.

3. Add the minced garlic and sauté for 1 to 2 more minutes until fragrant.
4. Add the rinsed lentils, diced tomatoes, dried oregano, dried thyme, vegetable broth, salt and black pepper.
5. Bring the soup to a boil, then reduce the heat to low, cover and simmer for 30-35 minutes or until the lentils are tender.
6. Taste and adjust seasoning as needed.
7. Serve hot, garnished with fresh parsley. Optionally, drizzle each serving with a splash of red wine vinegar.

Nutritional information (per serving):
Calories: 220 | Protein: 13g | Carbohydrates: 35g | Fat: 4g | Fiber: 9g

3. Pasta with Mediterranean Tomato Sauce

Introduction: Pasta with Mediterranean tomato sauce is a simple and tasty dish made with pasta and a rich tomato sauce with Mediterranean herbs and spices.

Prep time: 10 minutes | Cook time: 20 minutes | Yield: 4 servings

Ingredients:

- 8 ounces penne or spaghetti
- 2 tablespoons extra virgin olive oil
- 1 onion, finely chopped
- 2 cloves garlic, minced
- 1 can (14.5 ounces) diced tomatoes
- 1/2 teaspoon dried basil
- 1/2 teaspoon dried oregano
- 1/4 teaspoon red pepper flakes (adjust to taste)
- Salt and black pepper to taste
- Fresh basil leaves, to decorate.

- Grated Parmesan cheese, to serve (optional)

Method of Preparation

1. Cook pasta according to package directions until al dente. Drain and reserve.
2. In a large skillet, heat the extra virgin olive oil over medium heat.
3. Add finely chopped onion and sauté for 3-4 minutes until translucent.
4. Add the minced garlic and sauté for 1 to 2 more minutes until fragrant.
5. Add the diced tomatoes (with their juice), dried basil, dried oregano, red pepper flakes, salt, and black pepper. Stir to combine.
6. Simmer the sauce for 10 to 12 minutes, stirring occasionally, until it thickens and the flavors blend.
7. Serve the Mediterranean tomato sauce over cooked pasta.
8. Garnish with fresh basil leaves and grated Parmesan cheese if desired.

Nutritional information (per serving, without Parmesan cheese): Calories: 280 | Protein: 6g | Carbohydrates: 47g | Fat: 7g | Fiber: 4g

4. Spanakopita Greek Pasta

Introduction: Spanakopita Greek Pasta is a delicious fusion of traditional Spanakopita pasta and flavors. Combine spinach, feta cheese, and Mediterranean herbs with pasta for a satisfying dish.

Preparation time: 15 minutes | Cooking time: 15 minutes | Yield: 4 servings

Ingredients:

- 8 ounces penne or fusilli pasta
- 1 tablespoon extra virgin olive oil
- 1 onion, finely chopped
- 2 cloves garlic, minced
- 1 package (10 ounces) frozen chopped spinach, thawed and drained
- 1/2 cup crumbled feta cheese
- 1/4 cup chopped fresh dill
- 1/4 cup chopped fresh parsley
- Salt and black pepper to taste
- Lemon slices, to serve

Method of Preparation

1. Cook pasta according to package directions until al dente. Drain and reserve.
2. In a large skillet, heat the extra virgin olive oil over medium heat.
3. Add finely chopped onion and sauté for 3-4 minutes until translucent.
4. Add the minced garlic and sauté for 1 to 2 more minutes until fragrant.
5. Add the thawed and drained chopped spinach, crumbled feta cheese, chopped fresh dill, and chopped fresh parsley. Stir to combine and heat.
6. Season with salt and black pepper to taste.
7. Toss the cooked pasta with the spinach and feta mixture until well combined.
8. Serve hot with lemon wedges to squeeze over the pasta.

Nutritional information (per serving): Calories: 320 | Protein: 12g | Carbohydrates: 50g | Fat: 8g | Fiber: 5g

5. Mediterranean rice and beans

Introduction: Mediterranean rice and beans is a healthy and satisfying dish that combines rice, beans and Mediterranean spices. It is a comforting side or main dish.

Prep time: 10 minutes | Cook time: 25 minutes | Yield: 4 servings

Ingredients:

- 1 cup long grain white rice
- 2 cups of vegetable broth
- 1 can (15 ounces) white beans (such as cannellini beans), drained and rinsed
- 1/2 cup diced tomatoes (canned or fresh)
- 1/2 cup chopped red pepper
- 1/2 cup chopped green pepper
- 1/2 cup chopped red onion
- 2 cloves garlic, minced
- 2 tablespoons extra virgin olive oil
- 1 teaspoon dried oregano
- 1/2 teaspoon ground cumin
- Salt and black pepper to taste
- Fresh parsley, to decorate
- Lemon wedges, to serve (optional)

Method of Preparation

1. In a saucepan, combine long grain white rice and vegetable broth. Bring to a boil, then reduce heat to low, cover and simmer for 15 minutes or until rice is cooked and liquid is absorbed. Remove from heat and let cool.
2. In a large skillet, heat the extra virgin olive oil over medium heat.
3. Add minced garlic and sauté for 1-2 minutes until fragrant.
4. Add the diced red pepper, diced green pepper, diced red onion, and diced tomatoes. Sauté for 5-7 minutes until the vegetables begin to soften.
5. Add cooked rice, white beans, dried oregano, ground cumin, salt and black pepper. Stir to combine and heat.
6. Garnish with fresh parsley.
7. Serve hot with lemon wedges if desired.

Nutritional information (per serving, without lemon wedges): Calories: 300 | Protein: 9g | Carbohydrates: 55g | Fat: 6g | Fiber: 7g

6. Mediterranean chickpea stew

Introduction: Mediterranean chickpea stew is a hearty and tasty dish made with chickpeas, vegetables and Mediterranean spices. It is a nutritious and satisfying option as a main dish or side dish.

Prep time: 15 minutes | Cook time: 30 minutes | Yield: 4 servings

Ingredients:

- 2 cans (15 ounces each) chickpeas, drained and rinsed
- 1 onion, finely chopped
- 2 cloves garlic, minced
- 1 red bell pepper, diced
- 1 yellow bell pepper, diced
- 1 can (14.5 ounces) diced tomatoes
- 1 teaspoon ground cumin
- 1/2 teaspoon smoked paprika
- 1/4 teaspoon cayenne pepper (adjust to taste)
- 1/4 cup chopped fresh parsley
- 2 tablespoons extra virgin olive oil
- Salt and black pepper to taste

Method of Preparation

1. In a large skillet, heat the extra virgin olive oil over medium heat.
2. Add finely chopped onion and sauté for 3-4 minutes until translucent.
3. Add the minced garlic and sauté for 1 to 2 more minutes until fragrant.

4. Add the diced red pepper and the diced yellow pepper. Sauté for 5-7 minutes until the peppers begin to soften.
5. Add the drained and rinsed chickpeas, diced tomatoes (with their juice), ground cumin, smoked paprika, cayenne pepper (if using), salt, and black pepper.
6. Simmer the stew for 15 to 20 minutes, stirring occasionally, until the flavors blend and the stew thickens.
7. Garnish with fresh chopped parsley.
8. Serve hot as a main dish or side dish.

Nutritional information (per serving): Calories: 280 | Protein: 10g | Carbohydrates: 44g | Fat: 8g | Fiber: 11g

7. Lemon Orzo with Roasted Vegetables

Introduction: Lemon Orzo with Roasted Vegetables is a bright and flavorful dish that combines orzo pasta with a blend of roasted Mediterranean vegetables. It is a delicious side dish or light meal.

Prep time: 15 minutes | Cook time: 25 minutes | Yield: 4 servings

Ingredients:

- 1 cup orzo pasta
- 1 zucchini, diced
- 1 yellow bell pepper, diced
- 1 red bell pepper, diced
- 1 red onion, chopped
- 2 cloves garlic, minced
- 3 tablespoons extra virgin olive oil
- 2 tablespoons fresh lemon juice
- 1 teaspoon lemon zest
- 1 teaspoon dried oregano
- Salt and black pepper to taste

- Fresh basil leaves, to decorate.

Method of Preparation

1. Preheat oven to 425°F (220°C).
2. In a large bowl, toss diced zucchini, diced yellow bell pepper, diced red pepper, and diced red onion with 2 tablespoons extra virgin olive oil, minced garlic, dried oregano, salt, and black pepper.
3. Spread the seasoned vegetables in a single layer on a baking sheet.
4. Roast in the preheated oven for 20-25 minutes, or until the vegetables are tender and lightly caramelized. Stir them once or twice during roasting.
5. While the vegetables are roasting, cook the orzo pasta according to package directions until al dente. Drain and reserve.
6. In a large bowl, combine the cooked orzo pasta, roasted vegetables, fresh lemon juice, lemon zest, and 1 tablespoon extra virgin olive oil. Mix to combine.
7. Season with additional salt and black pepper to taste.
8. Garnish with fresh basil leaves.
9. Serve warm or at room temperature.

Nutritional information (per serving): Calories: 320 | Protein: 6g | Carbohydrates: 49g | Fat: 11g | Fiber: 5g

8. Broad bean dip (Foul Mudammas)

Introduction: Fava bean sauce, known as "Foul Mudammas", is a creamy and flavorful Middle Eastern sauce made with fava beans, lemon and Mediterranean spices. It is perfect for dipping bread or vegetables.

Prep time: 10 minutes | Cook time: 10 minutes | Yield: 4 servings

Ingredients:

- 2 cans (15 ounces each) fava beans, drained and rinsed
- 3 cloves garlic, minced
- 3 tablespoons extra virgin olive oil
- 2 tablespoons fresh lemon juice
- 1 teaspoon ground cumin
- 1/2 teaspoon paprika
- Salt and black pepper to taste
- Chopped fresh parsley, to decorate
- Sliced radishes, to serve (optional)
- Pita bread, for dipping

Method of Preparation

1. In a saucepan, combine the drained and rinsed fava beans, minced garlic, extra virgin olive oil, ground cumin, paprika, salt and black pepper.
2. Simmer, stirring occasionally, for 10 minutes until flavors blend and beans are heated through.
3. Remove from heat and let cool slightly.
4. Mash the bean mixture with a fork or potato masher to achieve the desired level of creaminess.
5. Add fresh lemon juice and adjust seasoning if necessary.
6. Transfer the bean sauce to a serving bowl.
7. Garnish with fresh chopped parsley.
8. Serve with sliced radishes and pita bread for dipping.

Nutritional information (per serving, without radishes and pita bread): Calories: 210 | Protein: 9g | Carbohydrates: 22g | Fat: 11g | Fiber: 7g

9. Greek pastitsio

Introduction: Greek pastitsio is a classic Greek baked pasta dish that includes layers of pasta, seasoned ground beef, and a creamy bechamel sauce. It is a comforting and indulgent Mediterranean recipe.

Prep time: 30 minutes | Cook time: 45 minutes | Yield: 8 servings

Ingredients:

For the Meat Sauce:

- 1 pound ground beef or lamb
- 1 onion, finely chopped
- 2 cloves garlic, minced
- 1 can (14.5 ounces) diced tomatoes
- 1/4 cup tomato paste
- 1 teaspoon ground cinnamon
- 1/2 teaspoon ground nutmeg
- Salt and black pepper to taste
- 2 tablespoons extra virgin olive oil

For the pasta:

- 1 pound penne or ziti pasta
- 2 tablespoons extra virgin olive oil
- 2 large eggs
- 1/2 cup grated Parmesan cheese

For the Béchamel Sauce:

- 4 cups of whole milk
- 1/2 cup unsalted butter
- 1/2 cup all-purpose flour
- 1/4 teaspoon ground nutmeg
- Salt and black pepper to taste
- 2 large eggs, beaten

Method of Preparation

For the Meat Sauce:

1. In a large skillet, heat 2 tablespoons extra virgin olive oil over medium heat.
2. Add finely chopped onion and sauté for 3-4 minutes until translucent.
3. Add the minced garlic and sauté for 1 to 2 more minutes until fragrant.
4. Add the ground beef or lamb and cook until browned, breaking it into small pieces as it cooks.
5. Add the diced tomatoes, tomato paste, ground cinnamon, ground nutmeg, salt and black pepper.
6. Simmer the sauce for 15-20 minutes until thickened. Remove from heat and set aside.

For the pasta:

7. Cook penne or ziti pasta according to package directions until al dente. Drain and mix with 2 tablespoons of extra virgin olive oil to prevent sticking. Let cool.

For the Béchamel Sauce:

8. In a saucepan, heat the whole milk until it is hot but not boiling. Keep it warm.
9. In a separate saucepan, melt unsalted butter over medium heat.
10. Add the all-purpose flour to make a roux. Cook for 2-3 minutes, stirring constantly, until the roux turns a light golden color.
11. Gradually add the hot milk, stirring constantly to avoid lumps.
12. Cook sauce for 5-7 minutes until thickened, stirring constantly.
13. Remove from heat and season with ground nutmeg, salt and black pepper.
14. Let the sauce cool slightly and then add the beaten eggs.

To assemble and bake:

15. 5Preheat oven to 350°F (175°C).
16. In a large bowl, combine the cooked pasta, 2 beaten eggs, and the grated Parmesan cheese. Toss to coat the pasta evenly.
17. Grease a 9x13-inch baking dish. Spread half of the pasta mixture evenly on the bottom of the plate.
18. Cover with meat sauce, distributing it evenly.
19. Add the remaining pasta mixture on top of the meat sauce.
20. Pour the bechamel sauce evenly over the top layer of pasta.
21. Bake in the preheated oven for 45-50 minutes, or until the top is golden brown and the pastitsio is set.
22. Let it cool for a few minutes before cutting and serving.

Nutritional information (per serving): Calories: 680 | Protein: 31g | Carbohydrates: 50g | Fat: 40g | Fiber: 2g

10. Mediterranean Bulgur Salad

Introduction: Mediterranean bulgur salad is a nutritious and tasty dish made with cooked bulgur wheat, fresh vegetables and Mediterranean herbs. It is a healthy and satisfying side dish or light meal.

Prep time: 20 minutes | Cook time: 15 minutes | Yield: 4 servings

Ingredients:

- 1 cup coarse bulgur wheat
- 2 cups of boiling water
- 1 cucumber, diced
- 1 tomato, diced
- 1/2 cup chopped red onion
- 1/4 cup chopped fresh parsley
- 1/4 cup chopped fresh mint
- 1/4 cup extra virgin olive oil
- 2 tablespoons fresh lemon juice

- Salt and black pepper to taste
- Crumbled feta cheese (optional)

Method of Preparation

1. Place the coarse bulgur wheat in a heatproof bowl and pour 2 cups of boiling water over it. Cover and let sit for 15 minutes, or until the bulgur is tender and has absorbed the water. Stir with a fork and let cool.
2. In a large bowl, combine the cooked bulgur, diced cucumber, diced tomato, diced red onion, chopped fresh parsley, and chopped fresh mint.
3. In a small bowl, whisk together the extra virgin olive oil, fresh lemon juice, salt, and black pepper.
4. Drizzle dressing over salad and toss to combine.
5. If desired, sprinkle with crumbled feta cheese.
6. Serve cold or at room temperature.

Nutritional information (per serving, without feta cheese): Calories: 330 | Protein: 6g | Carbohydrates: 46g | Fat: 14g | Fiber: 9g

11. Mediterranean White Bean Salad

Introduction: Mediterranean White Bean Salad is a vibrant, protein-rich dish that includes white beans, colorful vegetables, and Mediterranean flavors. It is a healthy and satisfying side or main dish.

Prep time: 15 minutes | Cook time: 0 minutes | Yield: 4 servings

Ingredients:

- 2 cans (15 ounces each) navy beans (such as cannellini beans), drained and rinsed
- 1 cup cherry tomatoes, cut in half
- 1/2 cup diced cucumber
- 1/2 cup chopped red onion
- 1/4 cup chopped fresh parsley
- 1/4 cup chopped fresh basil
- 1/4 cup extra virgin olive oil
- 2 tablespoons fresh lemon juice
- 2 cloves garlic, minced
- 1 teaspoon dried oregano
- Salt and black pepper to taste
- Crumbled feta cheese (optional)

Method of Preparation

1. In a large salad bowl, combine the drained and rinsed navy beans, cherry tomatoes, diced cucumber, diced red onion, chopped fresh parsley, and chopped fresh basil.
2. In a small bowl, whisk together the extra virgin olive oil, fresh lemon juice, minced garlic, dried oregano, salt, and black pepper.
3. Drizzle dressing over salad and toss to combine.
4. If desired, sprinkle with crumbled feta cheese.
5. Serve cold or at room temperature.

Nutritional information (per serving, without feta cheese): Calories: 320 | Protein: 10g | Carbohydrates: 40g | Fat: 15g | Fiber: 8g

12. Greek moussaka

Introduction: Greek moussaka is a classic Mediterranean casserole made with layers of eggplant, seasoned ground beef, and a creamy bechamel sauce. It is a hearty and indulgent dish.

Prep time: 45 minutes | Cook time: 1 hour | Yield: 6 servings

Ingredients:

For the eggplant layer:

- 2 large eggplants, cut into 1/2-inch slices
- Salt
- Olive oil for brushing

For the Meat Sauce:

- 1 pound ground beef or lamb
- 1 onion, finely chopped
- 2 cloves garlic, minced
- 1 can (14.5 ounces) diced tomatoes
- 2 tablespoons tomato paste
- 1 teaspoon ground cinnamon
- 1/2 teaspoon ground nutmeg
- Salt and black pepper to taste
- 2 tablespoons extra virgin olive oil

For the Béchamel Sauce:

- 4 cups of whole milk
- 1/2 cup unsalted butter
- 1/2 cup all-purpose flour
- 1/4 teaspoon ground nutmeg
- Salt and black pepper to taste
- 2 large eggs, beaten
- 1/2 cup grated Parmesan cheese

Method of Preparation

For the eggplant layer:

1. Place the eggplant slices in a colander and sprinkle each slice with salt. Let them sit for 30 minutes to release excess moisture.
2. Rinse the eggplant slices under cold water and pat dry with paper towels.
3. Preheat oven to 375°F (190°C).
4. Brush both sides of the eggplant slices with olive oil and place them on baking sheets in a single layer.

5. Roast in the preheated oven for 20-25 minutes, turning once, until the eggplant is tender and lightly browned. Remove from oven and set aside.

For the Meat Sauce:

6. In a large skillet, heat 2 tablespoons extra virgin olive oil over medium heat.
7. Add finely chopped onion and sauté for 3-4 minutes until translucent.
8. Add the minced garlic and sauté for 1 to 2 more minutes until fragrant.
9. Add the ground beef or lamb and cook until browned, breaking it into small pieces as it cooks.
10. Add the diced tomatoes, tomato paste, ground cinnamon, ground nutmeg, salt and black pepper.
11. Simmer the sauce for 15-20 minutes until thickened. Remove from heat and set aside.

For the Béchamel Sauce:

12. In a saucepan, heat the whole milk until it is hot but not boiling. Keep it warm.
13. In a separate saucepan, melt unsalted butter over medium heat.
14. Add the all-purpose flour to make a roux. Cook for 2-3 minutes, stirring constantly, until the roux turns a light golden color.
15. Gradually add the hot milk, stirring constantly to avoid lumps.
16. Cook sauce for 5-7 minutes until thickened, stirring constantly.
17. Remove from heat and season with ground nutmeg, salt and black pepper.
18. Let the sauce cool slightly, then add the beaten eggs and grated Parmesan cheese.

To assemble and bake:

19. Preheat oven to 350°F (175°C).
20. Grease a 9x13-inch baking dish.
21. Place half of the roasted eggplant slices on the bottom of the plate.

22. Cover with meat sauce, distributing it evenly.
23. Add the remaining roasted eggplant slices on top of the meat sauce.
24. Pour the bechamel sauce evenly over the top layer of eggplant.
25. Bake in the preheated oven for 45-50 minutes, or until the top is golden brown and the moussaka is firm.
26. Let it cool for a few minutes before cutting and serving.

Nutritional information (per serving): Calories: 600 | Protein: 24g | Carbohydrates: 32g | Fat: 42g | Fiber: 6g

13. Mediterranean Couscous with Chickpeas

Introduction: Mediterranean couscous with chickpeas is a quick and tasty dish that includes couscous, chickpeas and Mediterranean spices. It is a versatile side or main dish.

Prep time: 10 minutes | Cook time: 10 minutes | Yield: 4 servings

Ingredients:

- 1 cup couscous
- 1 cup vegetable broth
- 1 can (15 ounces) chickpeas, drained and rinsed
- 1/2 cup diced cucumber
- 1/2 cup chopped red pepper
- 1/4 cup chopped red onion
- 2 tablespoons chopped fresh parsley
- 2 tablespoons extra virgin olive oil
- 1 tablespoon fresh lemon juice
- 1 teaspoon ground cumin
- Salt and black pepper to taste
- Crumbled feta cheese (optional)

Method of Preparation

1. In a saucepan, bring the vegetable broth to a boil. Remove from heat and add couscous. Cover and let rest for 5 minutes.
2. Stir the cooked couscous with a fork and let it cool.
3. In a large bowl, combine the cooked couscous, chickpeas, diced cucumber, diced red pepper, diced red onion, and chopped fresh parsley.
4. In a small bowl, whisk together the extra virgin olive oil, fresh lemon juice, ground cumin, salt, and black pepper.
5. Drizzle dressing over couscous mixture and toss to combine.
6. If desired, sprinkle with crumbled feta cheese.
7. Serve cold or at room temperature.

Nutritional information (per serving, without feta cheese): Calories: 350 | Protein: 9g | Carbohydrates: 57g | Fat: 9g | Fiber: 8g

14. Lebanese Mujadara

Introduction: Lebanese mujadara is a comforting and healthy dish made with lentils, rice and caramelized onion. It is a staple in Lebanese cuisine.

Prep time: 10 minutes | Cook time: 45 minutes Yield: 4 servings

Ingredients:

- 1 cup brown or green lentils, rinsed and drained
- 1/2 cup long grain white rice

- 4 cups of water
- 1 onion, thinly sliced
- 3 tablespoons extra virgin olive oil
- 1 teaspoon ground cumin
- 1/2 teaspoon ground cilantro
- Salt and black pepper to taste
- Fresh parsley, to decorate
- Yogurt, to serve (optional)

Method of Preparation

1. In a large saucepan, combine the rinsed lentils and water. Bring to a boil, then reduce heat to low, cover and simmer for 20 minutes.
2. Add the long grain white rice, ground cumin, ground coriander, salt and black pepper. Cover and simmer for 20 to 25 minutes more, or until the rice and lentils are tender and the liquid has been absorbed. Remove from heat and let cool.
3. While the lentils and rice are cooking, heat 3 tablespoons of extra virgin olive oil in a skillet over medium heat.
4. Add the thinly sliced onion and sauté for 15 to 20 minutes, stirring frequently, until the onions are golden brown and caramelized.
5. To serve, pour the mujadara onto a plate and top with caramelized onions and fresh parsley.
6. If desired, serve with yogurt on the side.

Nutritional information (per serving, without yogurt): Calories: 350 | Protein: 12g | Carbohydrates: 57g | Fat: 10g | Fiber: 11g

15. Tomato and Olive Farro Salad

Introduction: Farro Salad with Tomato and Olives is a hearty and flavorful dish that combines farro, ripe tomatoes, salty olives, and Mediterranean herbs. It is a nutritious and satisfying side or main dish.

Prep time: 15 minutes | Cook time: 25 minutes | Yield: 4 servings

Ingredients:

- 1 cup farro
- 3 cups of water
- 1 cup cherry tomatoes, cut in half
- 1/2 cup Kalamata olives, pitted and sliced
- 1/4 cup chopped red onion
- 2 tablespoons chopped fresh basil
- 2 tablespoons chopped fresh parsley
- 2 tablespoons extra virgin olive oil
- 1 tablespoon fresh lemon juice
- Salt and black pepper to taste
- Crumbled feta cheese (optional)

Method of Preparation

1. In a saucepan, combine farro and water. Bring to a boil, then reduce heat to low, cover, and simmer for 20 to 25 minutes, or until farro is tender. Drain excess water and let cool.
2. In a large bowl, combine the cooked farro, halved cherry tomatoes, sliced Kalamata olives, chopped red onion, chopped fresh basil, and chopped fresh parsley.
3. In a small bowl, whisk together the extra virgin olive oil, fresh lemon juice, salt, and black pepper.
4. Drizzle dressing over salad and toss to combine.
5. If desired, sprinkle with crumbled feta cheese.
6. Serve cold or at room temperature.

Nutritional information (per serving, without feta cheese): Calories: 330 | Protein: 7g | Carbohydrates: 54g | Fat: 10g | Fiber: 9g

MEDITERRANEAN SANDWICHES, PIZZAS AND WRAPS

1. Greek Gyro Sandwich

Introduction: The Greek Gyro Sandwich is a classic and delicious Mediterranean dish featuring tender, seasoned meat (often lamb or beef) served in a warm pita with fresh vegetables and yogurt-based tzatziki sauce.

Prep time: 15 minutes | Cook time: 15 minutes | Yield: 4 sandwiches

Ingredients:

For the gyro meat:

- 1 pound thinly sliced gyro meat (lamb or beef)
- 2 teaspoons olive oil
- 1 teaspoon ground cumin
- 1 teaspoon ground coriander

- Salt and black pepper to taste

For tzatziki sauce:

- 1 cup Greek yogurt
- 1/2 cucumber, finely grated and drained
- 2 cloves garlic, minced
- 1 tablespoon fresh lemon juice
- 1 tablespoon fresh dill, chopped
- Salt and black pepper to taste

For assembly:

- 4 rounds of pita bread
- sliced tomatoes
- Sliced red onions
- Sliced cucumbers
- Lettuce leaves

Method of Preparation

1. In a skillet, heat the olive oil over medium-high heat. Add the gyro beef slices and season with ground cumin, ground coriander, salt, and black pepper. Cook until heated through and slightly crispy.
2. In a bowl, combine Greek yogurt, grated cucumber, minced garlic, fresh lemon juice, fresh dill, salt, and black pepper. Mix well to make the tzatziki sauce.
3. Heat the pita bread slices in the oven or on a griddle.
4. Assemble the sandwiches by placing gyro beef, sliced tomatoes, sliced red onions, sliced cucumbers, and lettuce leaves inside each pita bread.
5. Drizzle tzatziki sauce over fillings.
6. Roll up sandwiches, secure with aluminum foil or parchment paper, and serve.

Nutritional information (per sandwich): Calories: 450 | Protein: 28g | Carbohydrates: 40g | Fat: 19g | Fiber: 3g

2. Mediterranean vegetarian wrap

Introduction: The Mediterranean Veggie Wrap is a healthy and tasty combination of fresh vegetables, hummus, feta cheese and Mediterranean spices wrapped in a tortilla.

Prep time: 15 minutes | Cook time: 0 minutes | Yield: 4 rounds

Ingredients:

- 4 large whole wheat tortillas
- 1 cup of hummus
- 1 cucumber, sliced
- 1 red bell pepper, thinly sliced
- 1 cup cherry tomatoes, cut in half

- 1/2 cup Kalamata olives, pitted and sliced
- 1/2 cup crumbled feta cheese
- 2 tablespoons fresh parsley, chopped
- 1 teaspoon dried oregano
- Salt and black pepper to taste

Method of Preparation

1. Place the whole wheat tortillas on a clean surface.
2. Spread a generous portion of hummus on each tortilla.
3. Layer cucumber slices, red pepper slices, cherry tomatoes, Kalamata olives, crumbled feta cheese, fresh parsley, dried oregano, salt, and black pepper on each tortilla.
4. Fold up the sides of the tortilla and then roll it tightly to form a wrap.
5. Cut each wrapper in half diagonally, if desired, and serve.

Nutritional information (per wrapper): Calories: 350 | Protein: 10g | Carbohydrates: 42g | Fat: 15g | Fiber: 6g

3. Pita and falafel sandwich

Introduction: The Falafel Pita Sandwich is a vegetarian delight featuring crispy falafel balls, fresh vegetables and tahini sauce stuffed inside a warm pita bread.

Prep time: 20 minutes | Cook time: 15 minutes | Yield: 4 sandwiches

Ingredients:

For falafel:

- 1 can (15 ounces) chickpeas, drained and rinsed

- 1/4 cup chopped fresh parsley
- 1/4 cup chopped fresh cilantro
- 1/2 onion, chopped
- 2 cloves garlic, minced
- 1 teaspoon ground cumin
- 1 teaspoon ground coriander
- 1/4 teaspoon cayenne pepper
- Salt and black pepper to taste
- 1 teaspoon baking powder
- 4-6 tablespoons all-purpose flour
- Vegetable oil for frying

For tahini sauce:

- 1/2 cup tahini
- 2 tablespoons fresh lemon juice
- 1 clove garlic, minced
- Salt and black pepper to taste
- Water (to dilute, as needed)

For assembly:

- 4 rounds of pita bread
- sliced tomatoes
- Sliced cucumbers
- Sliced red onions
- Lettuce leaves

Method of Preparation

For falafel:

1. In a food processor, combine the chickpeas, chopped fresh parsley, chopped fresh cilantro, chopped onion, minced garlic, ground cumin, ground coriander, cayenne pepper, salt, black pepper, and powder. to bake. Pulse until the mixture is finely chopped and holds together.
2. Transfer the mixture to a bowl and add the all-purpose flour until the mixture can be formed into balls without sticking to your hands.
3. Form the mixture into balls or burgers.

4. Heat the vegetable oil in a skillet over medium-high heat. Fry the falafel balls or burgers until golden and crispy. Drain on paper towels.

For tahini sauce:

5. In a bowl, whisk together the tahini, fresh lemon juice, minced garlic, salt, and black pepper.
6. Add water little by little and beat until the sauce reaches the desired consistency. It should be smooth and pourable.

For assembly:

7. Heat the pita bread slices in the oven or on a griddle.
8. Spread tahini sauce on each pita bread.
9. Place the falafel, sliced tomatoes, sliced cucumbers, sliced red onions, and lettuce leaves inside each pita.
10. Drizzle with additional tahini sauce if desired.
11. Roll up sandwiches, secure with aluminum foil or parchment paper, and serve.

Nutritional information (per sandwich): Calories: 450 | Protein: 14g | Carbohydrates: 45g | Fat: 25g | Fiber: 7g

4. Mediterranean chicken pita

Introduction: Mediterranean Chicken Pita is a delicious combination of grilled chicken, fresh vegetables, olives, and feta cheese, all wrapped in warm pita bread and drizzled with tzatziki sauce.

Prep time: 20 minutes | Cook time: 15 minutes | Yield: 4 sandwiches

Ingredients:

For grilled chicken:

- 1 pound boneless, skinless chicken breasts
- 2 tablespoons olive oil
- 1 teaspoon dried oregano
- 1 teaspoon dried thyme
- Salt and black pepper to taste

For tzatziki sauce:

- 1 cup Greek yogurt
- 1/2 cucumber, finely grated and drained
- 2 cloves garlic, minced
- 1 tablespoon fresh lemon juice
- 1 tablespoon fresh dill, chopped
- Salt and black pepper to taste

For assembly:

- 4 rounds of pita bread
- sliced tomatoes
- Sliced red onions
- Sliced cucumbers
- Kalamata olives, pitted
- Crumbled feta cheese
- Fresh parsley, to decorate

Method of Preparation

For grilled chicken:

1. In a bowl, whisk together the olive oil, dried oregano, dried thyme, salt, and black pepper.
2. Coat the chicken breasts with the olive oil and herb mixture.
3. Grill the chicken on a hot grill or skillet for about 6 to 7 minutes per side or until cooked through. Let it sit for a few minutes and then cut it.

For tzatziki sauce:

4. In a bowl, combine Greek yogurt, grated cucumber, minced garlic, fresh lemon juice, fresh dill, salt, and black pepper. Mix well.

For assembly:

5. Heat the pita bread slices in the oven or on a griddle.
6. Spread tzatziki sauce on each pita bread.
7. Place sliced grilled chicken, sliced tomatoes, sliced red onions, sliced cucumbers, Kalamata olives, crumbled feta cheese, and fresh parsley inside each pita.
8. Drizzle with additional tzatziki sauce if desired.
9. Roll up sandwiches, secure with aluminum foil or parchment paper, and serve.

Nutritional information (per sandwich): Calories: 450 | Protein: 30g | Carbohydrates: 30g | Fat: 23g | Fiber: 3g

5. Pizza Margherita with a Mediterranean touch

Introduction: Margherita pizza with a Mediterranean touch is a fusion of the classic Italian Margherita pizza with Mediterranean flavors such as olives, feta cheese and fresh basil.

Prep time: 20 minutes | Cook time: 15 minutes | Yield: 2 pizzas (8 slices each)

Ingredients:

- 2 rounds pizza dough (store-bought or homemade)
- 1/2 cup pizza sauce
- 2 cups grated mozzarella cheese
- 1/2 cup Kalamata olives, pitted and sliced
- 1/2 cup crumbled feta cheese
- Fresh basil leaves, to decorate.
- Olive oil for drizzling
- Salt and black pepper to taste

Method of Preparation

1. Preheat your oven to the highest temperature it can reach (usually around 500°F or 260°C).
2. Roll out the pizza dough rounds on a floured surface to the desired thickness.
3. Transfer each rolled out dough to a pizza stone or baking sheet.
4. Spread the pizza sauce evenly over the dough, leaving a border for the crust.
5. Sprinkle shredded mozzarella cheese over the sauce.
6. Spread the Kalamata olives and crumbled feta cheese evenly over the pizza.
7. Season with a pinch of salt and black pepper.
8. Bake in the preheated oven for about 12-15 minutes, or until the crust is golden brown and the cheese is bubbly and lightly browned.
9. Remove from the oven, decorate with fresh basil leaves and drizzle with olive oil.
10. Cut and serve hot.

Nutritional information (per serving, based on 8 servings per pizza): Calories: 250 | Protein: 9g | Carbohydrates: 30g | Fat: 11g | Fiber: 1g

6. Mediterranean flatbread pizza

Introduction: Mediterranean Flatbread Pizza is a quick and easy pizza with a thin, crispy flatbread crust topped with Mediterranean-inspired ingredients like hummus, fresh vegetables, olives, and feta cheese.

Prep time: 15 minutes | Cook time: 10 minutes | Yield: 2 flatbread pizzas

Ingredients:

- 2 rounds flatbread (store-bought or homemade)
- 1/2 cup hummus
- 1 cup cherry tomatoes, cut in half
- 1/2 cup diced cucumber
- 1/4 cup sliced Kalamata olives
- 1/4 cup crumbled feta cheese
- Fresh parsley, to decorate
- Olive oil for drizzling
- Salt and black pepper to taste

Method of Preparation

1. Preheat your oven to 425°F (220°C).
2. Place the flatbread rounds on a baking sheet.
3. Spread a layer of hummus evenly over each flatbread, leaving a small border for the crust.
4. Place the halved cherry tomatoes, diced cucumber, sliced Kalamata olives, and crumbled feta cheese on top of the hummus.
5. Season with a pinch of salt and black pepper.
6. Bake in the preheated oven for about 8 to 10 minutes, or until the flatbreads are crispy and the ingredients are heated through.
7. Remove from the oven, garnish with fresh parsley and drizzle with olive oil.
8. Cut and serve immediately.

Nutritional information (per flatbread pizza): Calories: 300 | Protein: 10g | Carbohydrates: 36g | Fat: 14g | Fiber: 5g

7. Chicken and shawarma wrap

Introduction: The Chicken Shawarma Wrap is a flavorful and satisfying wrap featuring tender, spicy chicken, fresh vegetables, and creamy tahini sauce, all wrapped in a warm flatbread.

Prep time: 20 minutes | Cook time: 15 minutes | Yield: 4 rounds

Ingredients:

For Chicken Shawarma:

- 1 pound boneless, skinless chicken thighs
- 2 cloves garlic, minced
- 1 teaspoon ground cumin
- 1 teaspoon ground coriander
- 1/2 teaspoon ground paprika
- 1/4 teaspoon ground turmeric
- 1/4 teaspoon ground cinnamon
- Salt and black pepper to taste
- 2 tablespoons olive oil
- Juice of 1 lemon
- 4 large flatbreads or tortillas

For tahini sauce:

- 1/2 cup tahini
- 2 tablespoons fresh lemon juice
- 1 clove garlic, minced
- Salt and black pepper to taste
- Water (to dilute, as needed)

For assembly:

- Sliced cucumbers
- sliced tomatoes
- Sliced red onions
- Fresh parsley, chopped

Method of Preparation

For Chicken Shawarma:

1. In a bowl, combine minced garlic, ground cumin, ground coriander, ground paprika, ground turmeric, ground cinnamon, salt, black pepper, olive oil, and lemon juice.

2. Cut the chicken thighs into small pieces and add to the spice mixture. Toss to coat.
3. Heat a skillet over medium-high heat. Cook the marinated chicken pieces until cooked through and lightly browned.

For tahini sauce:

4. In a bowl, whisk together the tahini, fresh lemon juice, minced garlic, salt, and black pepper.
5. Add water little by little and beat until the sauce reaches the desired consistency. It should be smooth and pourable.

For assembly:

6. Heat flatbreads or large tortillas.
7. Spread a generous portion of tahini sauce over each flatbread.
8. Layer cooked chicken shawarma, sliced cucumbers, sliced tomatoes, sliced red onions, and fresh parsley on top of each flatbread.
9. Drizzle with additional tahini sauce if desired.
10. Roll up the wraps, secure with aluminum foil or parchment paper, and serve.

Nutritional information (per wrapper): | Calories: 450 | Protein: 25g | Carbohydrates: 30g | Fat: 25g | Fiber: 5g

8. Mediterranean vegetarian pizza

Introduction: Mediterranean Veggie Pizza is a vegetarian delight featuring a crispy pizza dough topped with a colorful array of fresh vegetables, olives, feta cheese, and garlic-herb olive oil.

Prep time: 20 minutes | Cook time: 15 minutes | Yield: 2 pizzas (8 slices each)

Ingredients:

- 2 rounds pizza dough (store-bought or homemade)
- 1/4 cup extra virgin olive oil
- 2 cloves garlic, minced
- 1 teaspoon dried oregano
- Salt and black pepper to taste
- 2 cups grated mozzarella cheese
- 1/2 cup cherry tomatoes, cut in half
- 1/2 cup sliced bell peppers (assorted colors)
- 1/2 cup sliced red onions
- 1/4 cup sliced Kalamata olives
- 1/4 cup crumbled feta cheese
- Fresh basil leaves, to decorate.

Method of Preparation

1. Preheat your oven to the highest temperature it can reach (usually around 500°F or 260°C).
2. Roll out the pizza dough rounds on a floured surface to the desired thickness.
3. Transfer each rolled out dough to a pizza stone or baking sheet.
4. In a bowl, combine the extra virgin olive oil, minced garlic, dried oregano, salt, and black pepper. Mix well to make the olive oil with garlic and herbs.
5. Brush the olive oil mixture over the pizza dough, covering the entire surface.
6. Sprinkle shredded mozzarella cheese evenly over the olive oil.
7. Scatter the halved cherry tomatoes, sliced bell peppers, sliced red onions, sliced Kalamata olives, and crumbled feta cheese evenly over the pizza.
8. Season with a pinch of salt and black pepper.
9. Bake in the preheated oven for about 12-15 minutes, or until the crust is golden brown and the cheese is bubbly and lightly browned.
10. Remove from the oven, decorate with fresh basil leaves and cut into slices.
11. Serve hot.

Nutritional information (per serving, based on 8 servings per pizza): Calories: 250 | Protein: 9g | Carbohydrates: 30g | Fat: 11g | Fiber: 2g

9. Turkey and hummus wrap

Introduction: The Turkey and Hummus Wrap is a tasty, protein-packed wrap that includes lean turkey, creamy hummus, fresh vegetables and Mediterranean seasonings, all wrapped in a tortilla.

Prep time: 15 minutes | Cook time: 0 minutes | Yield: 4 rounds

Ingredients:

- 4 large whole wheat tortillas
- 1 cup of hummus
- 1/2 pound sliced turkey breast
- Sliced cucumbers
- sliced tomatoes
- Sliced red onions
- fresh spinach leaves
- 1 teaspoon dried oregano
- Salt and black pepper to taste

Method of Preparation

1. Place the whole wheat tortillas on a clean surface.
2. Spread a generous portion of hummus on each tortilla.

3. Layer sliced turkey, sliced cucumbers, sliced tomatoes, sliced red onions, and fresh spinach leaves in each tortilla.
4. Sprinkle dried oregano, salt, and black pepper over the fillings.
5. Roll up the wraps, secure with aluminum foil or parchment paper, and serve.

Nutritional information (per wrapper): Calories: 350 | Protein: 18g | Carbohydrates: 40g | Fat: 14g | Fiber: 6g

10. Greek Chicken Pita Souvlaki

Introduction: Greek Chicken Souvlaki Pita is a delicious combination of marinated and grilled chicken skewers, fresh vegetables and tzatziki sauce wrapped in warm pita bread.

Prep time: 20 minutes | Cook time: 15 minutes | Yield: 4 sandwiches

Ingredients:

For chicken souvlaki:

- 1 pound boneless, skinless chicken breasts, cut into cubes
- 2 cloves garlic, minced
- 2 tablespoons extra virgin olive oil
- 1 teaspoon dried oregano
- 1 teaspoon dried thyme
- Juice of 1 lemon
- Salt and black pepper to taste

For tzatziki sauce:

- 1 cup Greek yogurt
- 1/2 cucumber, finely grated and drained
- 2 cloves garlic, minced
- 1 tablespoon fresh lemon juice
- 1 tablespoon fresh dill, chopped

- Salt and black pepper to taste

For assembly:

- 4 rounds of pita bread
- sliced tomatoes
- Sliced cucumbers
- Sliced red onions
- Fresh parsley, chopped

Method of Preparation

For chicken souvlaki:

1. In a bowl, combine minced garlic, extra virgin olive oil, dried oregano, dried thyme, lemon juice, salt, and black pepper.
2. Add the chicken cubes to the marinade and toss to coat. Let it marinate for at least 30 minutes, preferably longer.
3. Thread the marinated chicken cubes onto the skewers.
4. Grill the chicken skewers until cooked through and lightly charred.

For tzatziki sauce:

5. In a bowl, mix together Greek yogurt, grated cucumber, minced garlic, fresh lemon juice, fresh dill, salt, and black pepper. Mix well.

For assembly:

6. Heat the pita bread slices in the oven or on a griddle.
7. Spread tzatziki sauce on each pita bread.
8. Place the grilled chicken skewers, sliced tomatoes, sliced cucumbers, sliced red onions, and fresh parsley inside each pita.
9. Drizzle with additional tzatziki sauce if desired.
10. Roll up sandwiches, secure with aluminum foil or parchment paper, and serve.

Nutritional information (per sandwich): Calories: 450 | Protein: 30g | Carbohydrates: 30g | Fat: 23g | Fiber: 3g

11. Mediterranean Breakfast Pizza

Introduction: Mediterranean breakfast pizza is a delicious morning treat that includes a crispy pizza dough topped with scrambled eggs, fresh vegetables, olives and feta cheese.

Prep time: 20 minutes | Cook time: 15 minutes | Yield: 2 pizzas (8 slices each)

Ingredients:

- 2 rounds pizza dough (store-bought or homemade)
- 4 large eggs, beaten
- Salt and black pepper to taste
- 1/2 cup diced bell peppers (assorted colors)
- 1/2 cup chopped red onions
- 1/2 cup diced tomatoes
- 1/4 cup sliced Kalamata olives
- 1/2 cup crumbled feta cheese
- Fresh parsley, to decorate
- Olive oil for drizzling

Method of Preparation

1. Preheat your oven to the highest temperature it can reach (usually around 500°F or 260°C).
2. Roll out the pizza dough rounds on a floured surface to the desired thickness.
3. Transfer each rolled out dough to a pizza stone or baking sheet.
4. In a bowl, beat the eggs and season with salt and black pepper.
5. Heat a nonstick frying pan over medium heat and scramble the eggs until done.
6. Spread the scrambled eggs evenly over the pizza dough, leaving a border for the crust.
7. Evenly scatter the diced bell peppers, diced red onions, diced tomatoes, sliced Kalamata olives, and crumbled feta cheese over the eggs.
8. Bake in the preheated oven for about 12-15 minutes, or until the crust is golden brown and the ingredients are heated through.
9. Remove from the oven, garnish with fresh parsley and drizzle with olive oil.
10. Cut and serve hot.

Nutritional information (per serving, based on 8 servings per pizza): Calories: 200 | Protein: 8g | Carbohydrates: 20g | Fat: 10g | Fiber: 2g

12. Grilled Eggplant and Halloumi Sandwich

Introduction: The Grilled Eggplant and Halloumi Sandwich is a vegetarian delight that includes grilled eggplant, halloumi cheese, fresh vegetables, and a spicy dressing, all served on one sandwich.

Preparation time: 15 minutes | Cooking time: 15 minutes | Yield: 4 sandwiches

Ingredients:

For grilled eggplant and halloumi:

- 1 large eggplant, sliced
- 8 slices halloumi cheese
- 2 tablespoons extra virgin olive oil
- 1 teaspoon dried oregano
- Salt and black pepper to taste

For the Dressing:

- 1/4 cup extra virgin olive oil
- 2 tablespoons balsamic vinegar
- 1 clove garlic, minced
- Salt and black pepper to taste

For assembly:

- 4 ciabatta rolls or baguette halves
- sliced tomatoes
- fresh basil leaves
- fresh arugula leaves

Method of Preparation

For grilled eggplant and halloumi:

1. Preheat a grill or skillet over medium-high heat.
2. Brush both sides of the eggplant and halloumi cheese slices with olive oil.
3. Season the eggplant slices with dried oregano, salt and black pepper.
4. Grill the eggplant slices and halloumi cheese slices until tender and charred, about 3 to 4 minutes per side.

For the Dressing:

5. In a bowl, mix the extra virgin olive oil, balsamic vinegar, minced garlic, salt and black pepper. Mix well.

For assembly:

6. Divide ciabatta rolls or baguette halves.
7. Drizzle a generous amount of dressing on the bottom half of each roll.
8. Layer roasted eggplant slices, halloumi cheese slices, sliced tomatoes, fresh basil leaves, and fresh arugula leaves on top of the rolls.
9. Drizzle with additional dressing if desired.
10. Place top half of rolls over fillings to form sandwiches.
11. Serve immediately.

Nutritional information (per sandwich): Calories: 400 | Protein: 12g | Carbohydrates: 35g | Fat: 24g | Fiber: 4g

13. Mediterranean tuna wrap

Introduction: The Mediterranean Tuna Wrap is a protein-packed wrap that includes canned tuna, fresh vegetables, olives, and a tasty Mediterranean dressing, all wrapped in a tortilla.

Prep time: 15 minutes | Cook time: 0 minutes | Yield: 4 rounds

Ingredients:

- 4 large whole wheat tortillas
- 2 cans (5 ounces each) tuna in water, drained
- 1/2 cup diced cucumber
- 1/2 cup diced tomatoes
- 1/4 cup sliced Kalamata olives
- 1/4 cup crumbled feta cheese
- 2 tablespoons fresh parsley, chopped
- 2 tablespoons extra virgin olive oil
- 1 tablespoon fresh lemon juice
- 1 clove garlic, minced
- Salt and black pepper to taste

Method of Preparation

1. Place the whole wheat tortillas on a clean surface.
2. In a bowl, combine the canned tuna, diced cucumber, diced tomatoes, sliced Kalamata olives, crumbled feta cheese, and fresh parsley.
3. In a separate bowl, whisk together the extra virgin olive oil, fresh lemon juice, minced

garlic, salt, and black pepper to make the dressing.
4. Drizzle dressing over tuna mixture and toss to coat.
5. Pour the tuna mixture over each tortilla.
6. Roll up the wraps, secure with aluminum foil or parchment paper, and serve.

Nutritional information (per wrapper): Calories: 300 | Protein: 15g | Carbohydrates: 25g | Fat: 16g | Fiber: 4g

14. Mediterranean grilled cheese

Introduction: Mediterranean Grilled Cheese is a tasty take on the classic grilled cheese sandwich, featuring melted cheese, fresh tomatoes, Kalamata olives, and basil between two slices of crusty bread.

Prep time: 10 minutes | Cook time: 10 minutes | Yield: 2 sandwiches

Ingredients:

- 4 slices of bread (your choice)
- 4 ounces mozzarella cheese, sliced
- 2 small tomatoes, sliced
- 1/4 cup sliced Kalamata olives
- fresh basil leaves
- Olive oil for roasting

Method of Preparation

1. Place 2 slices of bread.
2. Layer mozzarella cheese slices, tomato slices, sliced Kalamata olives, and fresh basil leaves on each slice.
3. Top with remaining 2 slices of bread to make sandwiches.
4. Brush the outside of each sandwich with olive oil.

5. Heat a skillet over medium-high heat.
6. Grill sandwiches until golden brown and cheese is melted, about 3 to 4 minutes per side.
7. Cut and serve hot.

Nutritional information (per sandwich): Calories: 350 | Protein: 14g | Carbohydrates: 42g | Fat: 15g | Fiber: 4g

15. Mediterranean Vegetarian Quesadilla

Introduction: Mediterranean Vegetarian Quesadilla is a tasty fusion of Mexican and Mediterranean flavors, featuring a crispy tortilla filled with a tasty combination of vegetables, olives, feta cheese, and a creamy tzatziki sauce.

Prep time: 15 minutes | Cook time: 10 minutes | Yield: 2 quesadillas

Ingredients:

- 4 large whole wheat tortillas
- 1 cup diced bell peppers (assorted colors)
- 1/2 cup chopped red onions
- 1/2 cup sliced Kalamata olives
- 1/2 cup crumbled feta cheese
- 1/4 cup tzatziki sauce (store-bought or homemade)
- Olive oil for roasting

Method of Preparation

1. Place 2 tortillas on a clean surface.
2. On half of each tortilla, layer diced bell peppers, chopped red onions, sliced Kalamata olives, and crumbled feta cheese.
3. Drizzle tzatziki sauce over fillings.

4. Fold the other half of each tortilla over the fillings to create a half-moon shape.
5. Brush the outside of each quesadilla with olive oil.
6. Heat a skillet over medium-high heat.
7. Grill quesadillas until golden brown and cheese is melted, about 3-4 minutes per side.
8. Cut and serve hot.

Nutritional information (per quesadilla): Calories: 350 | Protein: 12g | Carbohydrates: 45g | Fat: 15g | Fiber: 6g

Enjoy these Mediterranean recipes for sandwiches, pizzas and wraps!

1. Grilled Mediterranean vegetables

Introduction: Grilled Mediterranean vegetables are a tasty and healthy side dish that captures the essence of Mediterranean cuisine with a combination of varied vegetables and Mediterranean spices.

Prep time: 15 minutes | Cook time: 15 minutes | Yield: 4 servings

Ingredients:

- 1 red pepper, cut into strips
- 1 yellow bell pepper, cut into strips
- 1 zucchini, sliced
- 1 eggplant, sliced
- 1 red onion, cut into rings
- 1/4 cup extra virgin olive oil
- 2 cloves garlic, minced
- 1 teaspoon dried oregano
- Juice of 1 lemon
- Salt and black pepper to taste
- Fresh parsley, to decorate

Method of Preparation

1. Preheat the grill to medium-high heat.
2. In a large bowl, combine the sliced vegetables.
3. In a separate bowl, whisk together the extra virgin olive oil, minced garlic, dried oregano, lemon juice, salt, and black pepper.
4. Drizzle the olive oil mixture over the vegetables and toss to coat evenly.
5. Place the vegetables on the grill and cook for about 5-7 minutes per side or until they have grill marks and are tender.
6. Remove from the grill, garnish with fresh parsley and serve hot.

Nutritional information (per serving): Calories: 150 | Protein: 2g | Carbohydrates: 10g | Fat: 12g | Fiber: 4g

2. Roasted Eggplant with Tahini

Introduction: Roasted Eggplant with Tahini is a classic Mediterranean appetizer that combines the smoky flavor of roasted eggplant with creamy tahini and a burst of fresh flavors.

Prep time: 10 minutes | Cook time: 30 minutes | Yield: 4 servings

Ingredients:

- 2 large eggplants
- 1/4 cup extra virgin olive oil
- 2 cloves garlic, minced
- 1/4 cup tahini
- Juice of 1 lemon
- Salt and black pepper to taste
- Fresh parsley, to decorate
- Pomegranate seeds, to decorate (optional)

Method of Preparation

1. Preheat your oven to 400°F (200°C).
2. Cut the eggplants in half lengthwise and mark the pulp in the shape of a cross.
3. Place the eggplant halves on a baking sheet, cut side up.
4. Drizzle the eggplants with extra virgin olive oil and season with salt and black pepper.
5. Roast the eggplants in the preheated oven for about 30 minutes or until tender and the skin charred.
6. Take the eggplants out of the oven and let them cool slightly.

7. In a bowl, combine minced garlic, tahini, and lemon juice. Mix well to make the tahini sauce.
8. Scoop out the flesh of the roasted eggplant and place on a serving platter.
9. Drizzle tahini sauce over eggplant.
10. Garnish with fresh parsley and pomegranate seeds (if using).
11. Serve hot as a sauce or spread.

Nutritional information (per serving): Calories: 180 | Protein: 4g | Carbohydrates: 15g | Fat: 12g | Fiber: 8g

3. Mushrooms stuffed with Greek spinach and feta cheese

Introduction: Spinach and Feta Stuffed Greek Mushrooms are a delicious appetizer that combines earthy mushrooms, sautéed spinach, and creamy feta cheese with Mediterranean seasonings.

Prep time: 20 minutes | Cook time: 25 minutes | Yield: 4 servings (8 stuffed mushrooms)

Ingredients:

- 8 large white button mushrooms, stemmed and reserved
- 1 cup fresh spinach, chopped
- 1/2 small red onion, finely chopped
- 2 cloves garlic, minced
- 1/4 cup crumbled feta cheese
- 2 tablespoons extra virgin olive oil
- 1 teaspoon dried oregano
- Salt and black pepper to taste
- Fresh parsley, to decorate

Preparation method

1. Preheat your oven to 375°F (190°C).
2. Clean the mushroom caps and remove the stems. Finely chop the mushroom stems.
3. In a frying pan, heat extra virgin olive oil over medium heat.
4. Sauté chopped mushroom stems, red onion, and garlic until softened, about 4 to 5 minutes.
5. Add the chopped spinach and cook until wilted, about 2 minutes.
6. Season the mixture with dried oregano, salt and black pepper.
7. Remove the pan from the heat and add the crumbled feta cheese.
8. Fill each mushroom cap with the spinach and feta mixture.
9. Place the stuffed mushrooms on a baking sheet.
10. Bake in the preheated oven for about 20-25 minutes or until the mushrooms are tender and the filling is golden.
11. Garnish with fresh parsley and serve hot.

Nutritional information (per serving - 2 stuffed mushrooms): Calories: 90 | Protein: 3g | Carbohydrates: 5g | Fat: 7g | Fiber: 2g

4. Mediterranean ratatouille

Introduction: Mediterranean Ratatouille is a vegetable mix that celebrates the flavors of the Mediterranean with tomatoes, eggplant, zucchini and a blend of herbs and spices.

Prep time: 20 minutes | Cook time: 40 minutes | Yield: 4 servings

Ingredients:

- 1 eggplant, diced
- 2 zucchini, diced
- 1 chopped onion
- 2 cloves garlic, minced
- 2 red peppers, diced
- 4 ripe tomatoes, diced
- 1/4 cup extra virgin olive oil
- 1 teaspoon dried thyme
- 1 teaspoon dried oregano
- Salt and black pepper to taste
- Fresh basil, to decorate

Method of Preparation

1. In a large skillet or pot, heat extra virgin olive oil over medium heat.
2. Add the chopped onion and sauté until translucent, about 3 minutes.
3. Add the minced garlic and cook for another minute.
4. Add the diced eggplant, zucchini and red peppers. Sauté for about 10 minutes until they start to soften.
5. Add the diced tomatoes, dried thyme, dried oregano, salt, and black pepper.
6. Reduce heat to low, cover, and simmer for about 30 minutes or until vegetables are tender and flavors blend.
7. Garnish with fresh basil and serve as a garnish.

Nutritional information (per serving): Calories: 180 | Protein: 3g | Carbohydrates: 19g | Fat: 11g | Fiber: 6g

5. Greek Lemon Roasted Potatoes

Introduction: Greek Lemon Roasted Potatoes are a classic Mediterranean side dish that features tender roasted potatoes with bright flavors of lemon, garlic, and Greek herbs.

Prep time: 15 minutes | Cook time: 45 minutes | Yield: 4 servings

Ingredients:

- 4 large russet potatoes, peeled and cut into wedges
- 1/4 cup extra virgin olive oil
- Juice of 2 lemons
- 4 cloves garlic, minced
- 1 teaspoon dried oregano
- Salt and black pepper to taste
- Fresh parsley, to decorate

Method of Preparation

1. Preheat your oven to 375°F (190°C).
2. In a large bowl, combine the potato slices, extra virgin olive oil, lemon juice, minced garlic, dried oregano, salt, and black pepper. Toss to coat the potatoes evenly.
3. Transfer potatoes to a baking dish in a single layer.
4. Roast in the preheated oven for about 40-45 minutes, or until the potatoes are golden brown and tender, turning once halfway through cooking.
5. Garnish with fresh parsley and serve hot.

Nutritional information (per serving) Calories: 320 | Protein: 5g | Carbohydrates: 46g | Fat: 14g | Fiber: 5g

6. Stuffed Peppers with Rice and Vegetables

Introduction: Stuffed Peppers with Rice and Vegetables is a satisfying Mediterranean dish that combines peppers, rice, and a tasty vegetable filling.

Prep time: 20 minutes | Cook time: 50 minutes | Yield: 4 servings (8 stuffed pepper halves)

Ingredients:

- 4 large bell peppers (red, yellow or green)
- 1 cup long-grain white rice, cooked
- 1/2 cup diced tomatoes
- 1/2 cup diced zucchini
- 1/2 cup chopped red onion
- 1/2 cup chopped eggplant
- 2 cloves garlic, minced
- 1/4 cup chopped fresh parsley
- 1 teaspoon dried oregano
- 1/4 cup extra virgin olive oil
- Salt and black pepper to taste
- Grated Parmesan cheese (optional)

Method of Preparation

1. Preheat your oven to 350°F (175°C).
2. Cut the tops off the bell peppers and remove the seeds and membranes. Set aside.
3. In a large skillet, heat the extra virgin olive oil over medium heat.
4. Add the chopped red onion, chopped eggplant and minced garlic. Sauté until softened, about 4 to 5 minutes.
5. Add the diced zucchini and diced tomatoes. Cook for 2-3 more minutes.
6. Remove the pan from the heat and add the cooked rice, chopped fresh parsley, dried oregano, salt and black pepper. Mix well.
7. Stuff the bell peppers with the rice and vegetable mixture.
8. Place the stuffed peppers in a baking dish.
9. Cover the dish with aluminum foil and bake in the preheated oven for about 30-35 minutes or until the peppers are tender.
10. Optionally, sprinkle grated Parmesan cheese on top before serving.

Nutritional information (per serving - 2 stuffed pepper halves): Calories: 320 | Protein: 5g | Carbohydrates: 48g | Fat: 12g | Fiber: 4g

7. Roasted Garlic Tomato Bruschetta

Nutritional information (per serving - 2 bruschetta): Calories: 220 | Protein: 4g | Carbohydrates: 26g | Fat: 11g | Fiber: 2g

Introduction: Roasted Garlic Tomato Bruschetta is a classic Mediterranean appetizer featuring roasted garlic cloves and fresh tomatoes on crusty toasted bread.

Prep time: 15 minutes | Cook time: 35 minutes | Yield: 4 servings (8 bruschetta)

Ingredients:

- 1 baguette, cut into 1/2-inch-thick slices
- 1 head of garlic
- 2 cups cherry tomatoes, cut in half
- 1/4 cup extra virgin olive oil
- 1/4 cup fresh basil leaves, chopped
- Salt and black pepper to taste
- Balsamic glaze for drizzling (optional)

Method of Preparation

1. Preheat your oven to 375°F (190°C).
2. Cut the top of the head of garlic to expose the cloves. Place it on a piece of aluminum foil, drizzle with a little olive oil and wrap.
3. Roast the garlic in the preheated oven for about 30-35 minutes, or until the cloves are soft and golden.
4. While the garlic is roasting, place the baguette slices on a baking sheet and toast them in the oven for about 5 minutes or until crispy.
5. Squeeze the roasted garlic cloves into a bowl and mash with a fork.
6. In another bowl, combine cherry tomatoes, extra virgin olive oil, chopped fresh basil, salt, and black pepper.
7. Spread roasted garlic paste over each toasted baguette slice.
8. Top with tomato mixture.
9. Optionally, drizzle with balsamic glaze before serving.

8. Mediterranean zucchini fritters

Introduction: Mediterranean Zucchini Fritters are crunchy, savory burgers made with grated zucchini, feta cheese and Mediterranean herbs, served with a refreshing yogurt sauce.

Prep time: 20 minutes | Cook time: 20 minutes | Yield: 4 servings (8 fritters)

Ingredients:

For zucchini fritters:

- 2 large zucchini, grated and squeezed to remove excess moisture
- 1/2 cup crumbled feta cheese
- 1/4 cup grated Parmesan cheese
- 1/4 cup chopped fresh dill
- 1/4 cup chopped fresh parsley
- 1/4 cup chopped green onions
- 2 cloves garlic, minced
- 2 large eggs
- 1/4 cup all-purpose flour
- 1 teaspoon baking powder
- Salt and black pepper to taste
- Olive oil for frying

For yogurt sauce:

- 1 cup Greek yogurt
- 1/2 cucumber, finely grated and drained
- 1 clove garlic, minced
- 1 tablespoon fresh lemon juice
- Salt and black pepper to taste

Method of Preparation

For zucchini fritters:

1. In a large bowl, combine the grated zucchini, crumbled feta cheese, grated Parmesan cheese, chopped fresh dill, chopped fresh parsley, chopped green onions, minced garlic, eggs, all-purpose flour, powder for baking, salt and black pepper. Mix well.
2. Heat a frying pan over medium-high heat and add enough olive oil to cover the bottom.
3. Drop spoonfuls of the zucchini mixture into the pan and flatten lightly with a spatula.
4. Cook for about 3-4 minutes per side or until the fritters are golden brown and cooked through.
5. Place the cooked fritters on paper towels to remove excess oil.

For yogurt sauce:

6. In a bowl, combine Greek yogurt, finely grated cucumber, minced garlic, fresh lemon juice, salt, and black pepper. Mix well.
7. Serve the Mediterranean zucchini fritters hot with the yogurt sauce on the side.

Nutritional information (per serving - 2 fritters with sauce): | Calories: 280 | Protein: 13g | Carbohydrates: 17g | Fat: 18g | Fiber: 2g

9. Greek-style green beans

Introduction: Greek-style green beans are a simple but tasty dish that includes tender green beans cooked with tomatoes, onions, garlic, and Mediterranean herbs.

Prep time: 15 minutes | Cook time: 30 minutes | Yield: 4 servings

Ingredients:

- 1 pound fresh green beans, sliced and halved
- 1/4 cup extra virgin olive oil
- 1 small onion, finely chopped
- 2 cloves garlic, minced
- 1 can (14 ounces) diced tomatoes
- 1 teaspoon dried oregano
- 1/2 teaspoon dried basil
- Salt and black pepper to taste
- Fresh parsley, to decorate
- Crumbled feta cheese (optional)

Method of Preparation

1. In a large skillet or pot, heat extra virgin olive oil over medium heat.
2. Add finely chopped onion and minced garlic. Sauté until onion is translucent, about 3 minutes.
3. Add the chopped and split green beans to the pan. Sauté for another 2-3 minutes.
4. Add the diced tomatoes, dried oregano, dried basil, salt and black pepper.
5. Reduce heat to low, cover, and simmer for about 25 to 30 minutes or until green beans are tender and flavors blend.
6. Garnish with fresh parsley and crumbled feta cheese (if using) before serving.

Nutritional information (per serving): Calories: 160 | Protein: 3g | Carbohydrates: 10g | Fat: 12g | Fiber: 4g

10. Roasted Beet Salad with Feta Cheese

Introduction: Roasted Beet Salad with Feta Cheese is a vibrant and nutritious Mediterranean salad that includes roasted beets, creamy feta cheese, and a savory vinaigrette dressing.

Prep time: 15 minutes | Cook time: 45 minutes | Yield: 4 servings

Ingredients:

- 4 medium beets, sliced and peeled
- 1/2 cup crumbled feta cheese
- 1/4 cup chopped fresh parsley
- 2 tablespoons extra virgin olive oil
- 1 tablespoon red wine vinegar
- 1 teaspoon Dijon mustard
- Salt and black pepper to taste
- Chopped walnuts to decorate (optional)

Method of Preparation

1. Preheat your oven to 375°F (190°C).
2. Cut the beets into small pieces.
3. Place the beet pieces on a baking tray, drizzle with a little extra virgin olive oil and season with salt and black pepper.
4. Roast the beets in the preheated oven for about 45 minutes or until tender.
5. In a bowl, combine the crumbled feta cheese and chopped fresh parsley.
6. In a separate bowl, whisk together the extra virgin olive oil, red wine vinegar, Dijon mustard, salt, and black pepper to make the vinaigrette.
7. Place the roasted beets on a serving platter.
8. Sprinkle the feta-parsley mixture over the beets.
9. Drizzle vinaigrette over salad.
10. Optionally, decorate with chopped walnuts before serving.

Nutritional information (per serving):
Calories: 200 | Protein: 5g | Carbohydrates: 16g | Fat: 14g | Fiber: 4g

11. Mediterranean Roasted Red Peppers

Introduction: Mediterranean Roasted Red Peppers are a versatile addition to your Mediterranean cooking repertoire. These roasted peppers are marinated with olive oil, garlic, and herbs for a touch of flavor.

Prep time: 10 minutes | Cook time: 25 minutes (roasting time) | Yield: 4 servings

Ingredients:

- 4 red peppers
- 1/4 cup extra virgin olive oil
- 2 cloves garlic, minced
- 1 teaspoon dried oregano
- Salt and black pepper to taste
- Fresh parsley, to decorate

Preparation method:

1. Preheat your oven to 450°F (230°C).
2. Cut the tops off the red peppers, remove the seeds and membranes and cut them into quarters.
3. Place the pepper quarters on a baking sheet, skin side up.
4. Roast the peppers in the preheated oven for about 25 minutes or until the skin is charred and blistered.
5. Remove the peppers from the oven and immediately cover them with a kitchen towel or place them in a sealed plastic bag. Let them steam for about 15 minutes.
6. Remove the skin from the roasted peppers and cut them into strips.
7. In a bowl, combine the extra virgin olive oil, minced garlic, dried oregano, salt, and black pepper. Mix well.
8. Pour the olive oil mixture over the roasted pepper strips.

9. Garnish with fresh parsley and serve as an appetizer or side dish.

Nutritional information (per serving): Calories: 130 | Protein: 1g | Carbohydrates: 8g | Fat: 11g | Fiber: 2g

12. Artichoke and olive tapenade

Introduction: Artichoke and olive tapenade is a tasty Mediterranean pasta that combines the salty flavors of artichokes and olives with aromatic herbs and garlic.

Prep time: 10 minutes | Cook time: 0 minutes | Yield: Approximately 1 cup

Ingredients:

- 1 cup pitted green olives
- 1 cup marinated artichoke hearts, drained
- 2 cloves garlic, minced
- 2 tablespoons extra virgin olive oil
- 1 tablespoon fresh lemon juice
- 1 teaspoon dried oregano
- Salt and black pepper to taste
- Fresh parsley, to decorate

Method of Preparation

1. In a food processor, combine pitted green olives, drained marinated artichoke hearts, minced garlic, extra virgin olive oil, fresh lemon juice, dried oregano, salt, and black pepper.
2. Pulse the mixture until it reaches the desired consistency, either chunky or smooth.
3. Taste and adjust seasonings if necessary.
4. Transfer the tapenade to a serving bowl, garnish with fresh parsley and serve.

Nutritional information (per 2 tablespoon serving): Calories: 40 | Protein: 1g | Carbohydrates: 2g | Fat: 3g | Fiber: 1g

13. Greek Roasted Eggplant Salad

Introduction: Greek Roasted Eggplant Salad is a vibrant dish featuring roasted eggplant, tomatoes, cucumbers, and a savory Greek dressing.

Prep time: 15 minutes | Cook time: 25 minutes | Yield: 4 servings

Ingredients:

- 2 medium eggplants, cut into cubes
- 1 cucumber, diced
- 2 tomatoes, diced
- 1/2 red onion, finely chopped
- 1/4 cup extra virgin olive oil
- 2 tablespoons red wine vinegar
- 1 teaspoon dried oregano
- Salt and black pepper to taste
- Fresh parsley, to decorate
- Kalamata olives (optional)

Method of Preparation

1. Preheat your oven to 425°F (220°C).
2. Place the cubed eggplant on a baking sheet, drizzle with a little extra virgin olive oil and season with salt and black pepper.
3. Roast the eggplant in the preheated oven for about 20-25 minutes or until tender and lightly browned.
4. In a bowl, combine the diced cucumber, diced tomatoes, finely chopped red onion, and roasted eggplant.
5. In a separate bowl, whisk together the extra virgin olive oil, red wine vinegar, dried

oregano, salt, and black pepper to make the dressing.
6. Drizzle dressing over salad and toss to coat evenly.
7. Garnish with fresh parsley and Kalamata olives (if using) before serving.

Nutritional information (per serving): Calories: 200 | Protein: 3g | Carbohydrates: 16g | Fat: 15g | Fiber: 5g

3. Drizzle the dressing over the salad and toss to coat the vegetables evenly.
4. Garnish with fresh basil leaves and crumbled feta cheese (if using) before serving.

Nutritional information (per serving): Calories: 150 | Protein: 2g | Carbohydrates: 10g | Fat: 12g | Fiber: 3g

14. Tomato and cucumber salad

Introduction: Tomato and Cucumber Salad is a light and refreshing Mediterranean salad that combines ripe tomatoes, crisp cucumbers, red onions, and a tangy vinaigrette dressing.

Prep time: 10 minutes | Cook time: 0 minutes | Yield: 4 servings

Ingredients:

- 4 ripe tomatoes, cut into wedges
- 1 cucumber, sliced
- 1/2 red onion, thinly sliced
- 1/4 cup extra virgin olive oil
- 2 tablespoons red wine vinegar
- 1 teaspoon dried oregano
- Salt and black pepper to taste
- Fresh basil leaves, to decorate.
- Feta cheese (optional)

Method of Preparation

1. In a large bowl, combine the tomato wedges, sliced cucumber, and thinly sliced red onion.
2. In a separate bowl, whisk together the extra virgin olive oil, red wine vinegar, dried oregano, salt, and black pepper to make the vinaigrette dressing.

15. Sautéed Kale with Lemon and Garlic

Introduction: Sautéed Kale with Lemon and Garlic is a quick and healthy Mediterranean side dish that features kale cooked with garlic, lemon, and a touch of red pepper flakes.

Prep time: 10 minutes | Cook time: 10 minutes | Yield: 4 servings

Ingredients:

- 1 bunch kale, stems removed and leaves chopped
- 2 tablespoons extra virgin olive oil
- 3 cloves garlic, minced
- Juice of 1 lemon
- A pinch of red pepper flakes (optional)
- Salt and black pepper to taste
- Grated Parmesan cheese to decorate (optional)

Method of Preparation

1. Heat extra virgin olive oil in a large skillet over medium heat.
2. Add the minced garlic and cook for about 1 minute until fragrant.
3. Add the chopped kale leaves to the pan and sauté for about 5 to 7 minutes, or until the kale is soft and tender.

4. Drizzle lemon juice over the kale and season with a pinch of red pepper flakes (if using), salt, and black pepper. Mix to combine.

5. Optionally, garnish with grated Parmesan cheese before serving.

Nutritional information (per serving): Calories: 90 | Protein: 3g | Carbohydrates: 7g | Fat: 7g | Fiber: 2g

1. Greek Chicken Souvlaki

Introduction: Greek chicken souvlaki is a classic Mediterranean dish known for its marinated and skewered chicken pieces, grilled to perfection and typically served with pita bread and tzatziki sauce.

Prep time: 20 minutes | Cook time: 15 minutes | Yield: 4 servings

Ingredients:

- 1.5 pounds boneless, skinless chicken breasts or thighs, cut into cubes
- 1/4 cup extra virgin olive oil
- 2 cloves garlic, minced
- 2 tablespoons fresh lemon juice
- 1 teaspoon dried oregano
- Salt and black pepper to taste
- Wooden skewers soaked in water.
- pita bread
- tzatziki sauce
- Sliced tomatoes, onions and cucumbers (optional, for garnish)

Method of Preparation

1. In a bowl, combine the extra virgin olive oil, minced garlic, fresh lemon juice, dried oregano, salt, and black pepper.
2. Add the chicken cubes to the marinade and toss to coat. Cover and refrigerate for at least 30 minutes or, ideally, marinate overnight.
3. Preheat a grill or skillet over medium-high heat.
4. Thread the marinated chicken cubes onto the soaked wooden skewers.
5. Grill the chicken skewers for about 12 to 15 minutes, turning occasionally, until cooked through and have grill marks.
6. Heat the pita bread on the grill for a minute or two.

7. Serve the chicken souvlaki with pita bread, tzatziki sauce, and optional sliced tomatoes, onions, and cucumbers.

Nutritional information (per serving, excluding optional garnishes): Calories: 300 | Protein: 30g | Carbohydrates: 10g | Fat: 15g | Fiber: 2g

2. Grilled Mediterranean Lamb Chops

Introduction: Grilled Mediterranean Lamb Chops are a succulent and flavorful dish that features lamb chops marinated and grilled to perfection with Mediterranean spices.

Prep time: 15 minutes | Cook time: 10 minutes | Yield: 4 servings

Ingredients:

- 8 lamb chops
- 1/4 cup extra virgin olive oil
- 2 cloves garlic, minced
- 1 tablespoon fresh lemon juice
- 1 teaspoon dried rosemary
- 1 teaspoon dried oregano
- Salt and black pepper to taste
- Fresh mint leaves, to decorate.

Method of Preparation

1. In a bowl, combine extra virgin olive oil, minced garlic, fresh lemon juice, dried rosemary, dried oregano, salt, and black pepper.
2. Place the lamb chops on a shallow plate and pour the marinade over them. Turn to coat lamb chops evenly. Cover and refrigerate for at least 30 minutes.
3. Preheat the grill to medium-high heat.

4. Grill the lamb chops for about 4-5 minutes per side over medium heat, or adjust the cooking time to your desired level of doneness.
5. Remove the lamb chops from the grill, cover them with aluminum foil, and let them rest a few minutes before serving.
6. Garnish with fresh mint leaves and serve.

Nutritional information (per serving): Calories: 350 | Protein: 24g | Carbohydrates: 1g | Fat: 28g | Fiber: 0g

3. Moroccan Chicken Tagine

Introduction: Moroccan chicken tagine is a tasty and aromatic stew cooked with chicken, spices and a mixture of vegetables, usually served with couscous or bread.

Preparation time: 20 minutes | Cooking time: 1 hour | Yield: 4 servings

Ingredients:

- 4 chicken thighs and 4 chicken drumsticks
- 2 tablespoons olive oil
- 1 onion, finely chopped
- 2 cloves garlic, minced
- 1 teaspoon ground cumin
- 1 teaspoon ground coriander
- 1 teaspoon ground cinnamon
- 1/2 teaspoon ground paprika
- 1/2 teaspoon ground ginger
- 1/2 teaspoon ground turmeric
- 1/4 teaspoon cayenne pepper (adjust to taste)
- 1 cup chicken broth
- 1 cup diced tomatoes (canned or fresh)
- 1 cup chopped carrots
- 1 cup diced bell peppers

- 1/2 cup pitted green olives
- 1/4 cup chopped fresh cilantro
- Salt and black pepper to taste
- Cooked couscous or bread, to serve

Method of Preparation

1. Heat the olive oil in a large tagine or heavy-bottomed pot with a lid over medium-high heat.
2. Add the chopped onion and garlic and sauté until softened, about 2-3 minutes.
3. Add the chicken thighs and drumsticks and brown on all sides, about 5 to 7 minutes.
4. Add the ground cumin, ground coriander, ground cinnamon, ground paprika, ground ginger, ground turmeric, and cayenne pepper. Cook for another 2 minutes until fragrant.
5. Pour in the chicken broth and diced tomatoes. Bring to a simmer.
6. Add chopped carrots, diced bell peppers, and pitted green olives.
7. Cover the tagine or pot with a lid and simmer for about 30 to 40 minutes, or until the chicken is cooked through and tender.
8. Season with salt and black pepper to taste.
9. Garnish with fresh chopped cilantro before serving.
10. Serve Moroccan Chicken Tagine with cooked couscous or bread.

Nutritional information (per serving, excluding couscous or bread): Calories: 350 | Protein: 30g | Carbohydrates: 12g | Fat: 20g | Fiber: 4g

4. Greek Lemon Garlic Chicken

Introduction: Greek Lemon Garlic Chicken is a simple but flavorful Mediterranean dish that features chicken marinated with tangy lemon and garlic and then roasted to perfection.

Prep time: 10 minutes | Cook time: 40 minutes | Yield: 4 servings

Ingredients:

- 4 chicken thighs with bone and skin
- 4 chicken thighs with bone and skin
- 1/4 cup extra virgin olive oil
- Juice of 2 lemons
- 4 cloves garlic, minced
- 1 teaspoon dried oregano
- Salt and black pepper to taste
- Fresh oregano leaves, to decorate (optional)

Method of Preparation

1. In a bowl, combine the extra virgin olive oil, lemon juice, minced garlic, dried oregano, salt, and black pepper.
2. Place the chicken thighs and drumsticks in a shallow dish and pour the marinade over them. Turn to coat chicken pieces evenly. Cover and refrigerate for at least 30 minutes.
3. Preheat your oven to 375°F (190°C).
4. Transfer the marinated chicken pieces to a baking dish, skin side up.
5. Roast in the preheated oven for about 35-40 minutes, or until the chicken is cooked through and the skin is crispy and golden.
6. Optionally, garnish with fresh oregano leaves before serving.

Nutritional information (per serving): Calories: 400 | Protein: 26g | Carbohydrates: 2g | Fat: 32g | Fiber: 1g

5. Turkish Kofte (Spiced Meatballs)

Introduction: Turkish kofte, also known as spiced meatballs, is a beloved Mediterranean dish made with ground meat mixed with flavorful spices and herbs, and usually served with pita bread or rice.

Prep time: 20 minutes | Cook time: 15 minutes | Yield: 4 servings

Ingredients:

- 1 pound ground beef or lamb
- 1 onion, finely grated
- 2 cloves garlic, minced
- 1/4 cup chopped fresh parsley
- 1 teaspoon ground cumin
- 1 teaspoon ground paprika
- 1/2 teaspoon ground cinnamon
- Salt and black pepper to taste
- Olive oil for frying
- Pita bread or rice, to serve
- Sliced tomatoes, onions and cucumbers (optional, for garnish)

Method of Preparation

1. In a large bowl, combine the ground beef or lamb, finely grated onion, minced garlic, minced fresh parsley, ground cumin, ground paprika, ground cinnamon, salt, and black pepper.
2. Mix the ingredients until well combined.
3. Form the meat mixture into small meatballs or patties.
4. Heat the olive oil in a skillet over medium-high heat.
5. Fry the meatballs or burgers for about 3-4 minutes per side, or until cooked through and golden brown.
6. Remove from the pan and drain on paper towels.
7. Serve Turkish Kofte with pita bread or rice and optionally sliced tomatoes, onions and cucumbers.

Nutritional information (per serving, excluding optional garnishes): Calories: 280 | Protein: 18g | Carbohydrates: 4g | Fat: 21g | Fiber: 1g

6. Mediterranean beef skewers

Introduction: Mediterranean beef kebabs are delicious skewers of marinated pieces of beef, grilled to perfection and served with a variety of Mediterranean side dishes and sauces.

Prep time: 20 minutes | Cook time: 10 minutes | Yield: 4 servings

Ingredients:

- 1 pound beef sirloin or tenderloin, cut into 1-inch cubes
- 1/4 cup extra virgin olive oil
- 2 cloves garlic, minced
- 1 tablespoon fresh lemon juice
- 1 teaspoon dried oregano
- 1 teaspoon ground cumin
- Salt and black pepper to taste
- Wooden skewers soaked in water.
- Tzatziki sauce or chimichurri sauce, for dipping

Method of Preparation

1. In a bowl, combine extra virgin olive oil, minced garlic, fresh lemon juice, dried oregano, ground cumin, salt, and black pepper.
2. Add the beef cubes to the marinade and toss to coat. Cover and refrigerate for at least 30 minutes.
3. Preheat the grill to medium-high heat.
4. Thread the marinated meat cubes onto the soaked wooden skewers.

5. Grill the meat skewers for about 3 to 4 minutes per side over medium heat, or adjust the cooking time to your desired doneness level.
6. Remove from the grill and serve with tzatziki sauce or chimichurri sauce for dipping.

Nutritional information (per serving, excluding sauce): Calories: 300 | Protein: 25g | Carbohydrates: 2g | Fat: 21g | Fiber: 0g

7. Spanish chicken and chorizo paella

Introduction: Spanish chicken and chorizo paella is a rich and flavorful one-pan dish that includes chicken, chorizo, rice, and a blend of spices.

Prep time: 20 minutes | Cook time: 35 minutes | Yield: 4 servings

Ingredients:

- 4 chicken thighs with bone and skin
- 6 ounces chorizo, sliced
- 1 chopped onion
- 1 red pepper, chopped
- 1 yellow pepper, chopped
- 2 cloves garlic, minced
- 1 1/2 cups arborio rice
- 1/2 teaspoon smoked paprika
- 1/2 teaspoon saffron threads (optional)
- 4 cups chicken broth
- 1 cup frozen peas
- Lemon wedges, to decorate
- Fresh parsley, to decorate
- Salt and black pepper to taste

Method of Preparation

1. Heat a large, deep skillet or paella pan over medium-high heat.
2. Add chicken thighs, skin side down, and cook until golden brown, about 5 minutes per side. Remove chicken from pan and set aside.
3. In the same skillet, add the sliced chorizo and cook until it begins to brown, about 2 minutes. Remove the chorizo and reserve.
4. In the same pan, add the chopped onion, red pepper, and yellow pepper. Sauté until vegetables soften, about 3 to 4 minutes.
5. Add the minced garlic and Arborio rice. Cook for another 2 minutes until the rice is lightly toasted.
6. Add smoked paprika and saffron strands (if using) and return the browned chicken and chorizo to the pan.
7. Pour in the chicken broth and bring to a simmer.
8. Reduce the heat to low, cover the pan and cook for about 20-25 minutes, or until the rice is tender and the chicken is cooked through.
9. Add frozen peas and cook for 2 more minutes or until heated through.
10. Season with salt and black pepper to taste.
11. Garnish with lemon wedges and fresh parsley before serving.

Nutritional information (per serving): Calories: 550 | Protein: 35g | Carbohydrates: 50g | Fat: 23g | Fiber: 3g

8. Lamb Shawarma

Introduction: Lamb Shawarma is a popular Mediterranean street food that includes thinly sliced marinated lamb, usually served in pita bread with tahini sauce and vegetables.

Prep time: 20 minutes | Cook time: 15 minutes | Yield: 4 servings

Ingredients:

- 1 pound boneless lamb leg or shoulder, thinly sliced
- 1/4 cup plain Greek yogurt
- 2 cloves garlic, minced
- 1 teaspoon ground cumin
- 1 teaspoon ground coriander
- 1/2 teaspoon ground paprika
- 1/2 teaspoon ground cinnamon
- 1/4 teaspoon cayenne pepper
- Salt and black pepper to taste
- olive oil for cooking
- pita bread
- tahini sauce
- Sliced cucumbers, tomatoes and onions (optional, for garnish)

Method of Preparation

1. In a bowl, combine plain Greek yogurt, minced garlic, ground cumin, ground coriander, ground paprika, ground cinnamon, cayenne pepper, salt, and black pepper.
2. Add the thinly sliced lamb to the marinade and toss to coat. Cover and refrigerate for at least 30 minutes.
3. Heat a frying pan over medium-high heat and add a little olive oil.
4. Cook the marinated lamb slices in batches for approximately 2-3 minutes per side, or until golden brown and cooked to your desired level of doneness.
5. Heat the pita bread in the pan for a minute or two.
6. Serve the Lamb Shawarma in pita bread with tahini sauce and, optionally, sliced cucumber, tomato and onion.

Nutritional information (per serving, excluding optional garnishes): Calories: 400 |

Protein: 30g | Carbohydrates: 10g | Fat: 25g | Fiber: 1g

9. Mediterranean Italian Pork Chops

Introduction: Italian Mediterranean Pork Chops are succulent pork chops seasoned with Mediterranean herbs and spices, usually served with a side of roasted vegetables or salad.

Prep time: 15 minutes | Cook time: 20 minutes Yield: 4 servings

Ingredients:

- 4 bone-in pork chops
- 1/4 cup extra virgin olive oil
- 2 cloves garlic, minced
- 1 tablespoon chopped fresh rosemary
- 1 tablespoon chopped fresh thyme
- 1 teaspoon dried oregano
- 1/2 teaspoon dried basil
- Salt and black pepper to taste
- Lemon wedges, to decorate
- Roasted vegetables or salad, to serve

Method of Preparation

1. In a bowl, combine extra virgin olive oil, minced garlic, minced fresh rosemary, minced fresh thyme, dried oregano, dried basil, salt, and black pepper.
2. Rub the pork chops with the prepared mixture of herbs and spices.
3. Preheat a grill or skillet over medium-high heat.

4. Grill the pork chops for about 8 to 10 minutes per side, or until they are cooked through and have grill marks.
5. Remove from the grill, let it rest for a few minutes and decorate with lemon slices.
6. Serve Italian Mediterranean Pork Chops with your choice of grilled vegetables or salad.

Nutritional information (per serving, excluding sides): Calories: 300 | Protein: 25g | Carbohydrates: 2g | Fat: 20g | Fiber: 1g

10. Moroccan lamb stew

Introduction: Moroccan lamb stew is a hearty and aromatic stew made with tender pieces of lamb, vegetables, nuts and a blend of Moroccan spices.

Prep time: 20 minutes | Cook time: 2 hours | Yield: 6 servings

Ingredients:

- 2 pounds boneless stewed lamb, cut into cubes
- 2 tablespoons olive oil
- 1 chopped onion
- 2 cloves garlic, minced
- 1 teaspoon ground cumin
- 1 teaspoon ground coriander
- 1/2 teaspoon ground cinnamon
- 1/4 teaspoon ground ginger
- 1/4 teaspoon ground paprika
- 1/4 teaspoon cayenne pepper (adjust to taste)
- Salt and black pepper to taste
- 2 cups diced tomatoes (canned or fresh)
- 4 cups beef or lamb broth
- 1 cup dried apricots, chopped
- 1 cup chickpeas (canned or cooked)
- 1/4 cup chopped fresh cilantro
- Couscous or cooked rice, to serve

Method of Preparation

1. In a large pot, heat the olive oil over medium-high heat.
2. Add the chopped onion and sauté until softened, about 2-3 minutes.
3. Add the minced garlic and lamb cubes. Brown the lamb on all sides, about 5 to 7 minutes.
4. Add ground cumin, ground coriander, ground cinnamon, ground ginger, ground paprika, cayenne pepper, salt and black pepper. Cook for another 2 minutes until fragrant.
5. Pour in the diced tomatoes and beef or lamb broth. Bring to a simmer.
6. Cover the pot, reduce the heat to low, and let the stew simmer for about 1.5 to 2 hours, or until the lamb is tender.
7. Add the dried apricots and chopped chickpeas. Cook for 15 more minutes.
8. Season with salt and black pepper to taste.
9. Garnish with fresh chopped cilantro.
10. Serve Moroccan lamb stew over couscous or cooked rice.

Nutritional information (per serving, excluding couscous or rice): Calories: 450 | Protein: 30g | Carbohydrates: 30g | Fat: 20g | Fiber: 6g

11. Greek moussaka with ground meat

Introduction: Greek Moussaka with Ground Beef is a classic Mediterranean casserole consisting of layers of ground beef, eggplant, potatoes, and a creamy bechamel sauce.

Prep time: 30 minutes | Cooking time: 1 hour | Yield: 6 servings

Ingredients:

- 1 pound of ground beef
- 2 eggplants, sliced
- 2 potatoes, peeled and cut into slices
- 1 onion, finely chopped
- 2 cloves garlic, minced
- 1 can (14 ounces) diced tomatoes
- 1/2 cup red wine (optional)
- 1 teaspoon ground cinnamon
- 1/2 teaspoon ground allspice
- Salt and black pepper to taste
- Olive oil for frying

For the bechamel sauce:

- 4 tablespoons unsalted butter
- 1/4 cup all-purpose flour
- 2 cups of milk
- 1/4 teaspoon ground nutmeg
- Salt and black pepper to taste
- Grated Parmesan cheese, to cover

Method of Preparation

1. Preheat your oven to 350°F (175°C).
2. Heat the olive oil in a skillet over medium-high heat.
3. Add the sliced eggplants and potatoes and fry until lightly golden. Remove and drain on paper towels.
4. In the same pan, add the chopped onion and minced garlic. Sauté until softened, about 2-3 minutes.
5. Add the ground beef and cook until browned, breaking it up with a spoon.
6. Add the diced tomatoes, red wine (if using), ground cinnamon, ground allspice, salt, and black pepper. Simmer for 10 minutes.
7. For the bechamel sauce, melt the butter in a saucepan over medium heat. Add the all-

purpose flour and cook for 2-3 minutes until a paste forms.
8. Gradually add the milk until the sauce thickens.
9. Season the bechamel sauce with ground nutmeg, salt and black pepper.
10. In a greased baking dish, layer half the eggplant and potato slices, followed by the ground beef mixture. Repeat with the remaining eggplants and potatoes.
11. Pour the bechamel sauce over the top and spread it evenly.
12. Sprinkle grated Parmesan cheese on top.
13. Bake in the preheated oven for 45 minutes to 1 hour, or until the moussaka is golden and bubbly.
14. Let it rest for a few minutes before serving.

Nutritional information (per serving): Calories: 450 | Protein: 20g | Carbohydrates: 30g | Fat: 25g | Fiber: 6g

12. Lebanese Chicken Shawarma

Introduction: Lebanese chicken shawarma is a tasty street food dish that includes marinated and roasted chicken, usually served in pita bread with garlic sauce and vegetables.

Prep time: 20 minutes | Cook time: 25 minutes | Yield: 4 servings

Ingredients:

- 1 pound boneless, skinless chicken thighs
- 1/4 cup plain Greek yogurt
- 2 cloves garlic, minced
- 2 teaspoons ground cumin
- 1 teaspoon ground coriander
- 1/2 teaspoon ground paprika
- 1/4 teaspoon ground cinnamon

- 1/4 teaspoon cayenne pepper (adjust to taste)
- Salt and black pepper to taste
- olive oil for cooking
- pita bread
- Garlic sauce or tahini sauce
- Sliced cucumbers, tomatoes and onions (optional, for garnish)

Method of Preparation

1. In a bowl, combine plain Greek yogurt, minced garlic, ground cumin, ground coriander, ground paprika, ground cinnamon, cayenne pepper, salt, and black pepper.
2. Add the chicken thighs to the marinade and toss to coat. Cover and refrigerate for at least 30 minutes.
3. Preheat a grill or skillet over medium-high heat.
4. Grill chicken thighs for about 4-5 minutes per side, or until cooked through and have grill marks.
5. Remove from the grill and let rest for a few minutes before cutting.
6. Heat the pita bread on the grill for a minute or two.
7. Serve Lebanese Chicken Shawarma in pita bread with garlic sauce or tahini sauce and, optionally, sliced cucumber, tomato and onion.

Nutritional information (per serving, excluding optional garnishes): Calories: 300 | Protein: 25g | Carbohydrates: 10g | Fat: 15g | Fiber: 1g

13. Mediterranean Pork Souvlaki

Introduction: Mediterranean pork souvlaki is a delicious dish featuring marinated and skewered pork, grilled to perfection and usually served with pita bread and tzatziki sauce.

Prep time: 20 minutes | Cook time: 15 minutes | Yield: 4 servings

Ingredients:

- 1.5 pounds boneless pork loin, cut into cubes
- 1/4 cup extra virgin olive oil
- 2 cloves garlic, minced
- 2 tablespoons fresh lemon juice
- 1 teaspoon dried oregano
- Salt and black pepper to taste
- Wooden skewers soaked in water.
- pita bread
- tzatziki sauce
- Sliced tomatoes, onions and cucumbers (optional, for garnish)

Method of Preparation

1. In a bowl, combine the extra virgin olive oil, minced garlic, fresh lemon juice, dried oregano, salt, and black pepper.
2. Add the pork cubes to the marinade and toss to coat. Cover and refrigerate for at least 30 minutes or, ideally, marinate overnight.
3. Preheat a grill or skillet over medium-high heat.
4. Thread the marinated pork cubes onto the soaked wooden skewers.
5. Grill the pork souvlaki for about 12 to 15 minutes, turning occasionally, until cooked through and has grill marks.
6. Heat the pita bread on the grill for a minute or two.
7. Serve the pork souvlaki with pita bread, tzatziki sauce, and optional sliced tomatoes, onions, and cucumbers.

Nutritional information (per serving, excluding optional garnishes): Calories: 350 | Protein: 30g | Carbohydrates: 10g | Fat: 20g | Fiber: 1g

14. Italian Mediterranean Meatballs

Introduction: Italian Mediterranean Meatballs are savory meatballs made with a mixture of ground beef and ground lamb, seasoned with Mediterranean herbs and spices.

Prep time: 20 minutes | Cook time: 20 minutes | Yield: 4 servings

Ingredients:

- 1/2 pound ground beef
- 1/2 pound ground lamb
- 1/4 cup breadcrumbs
- 1/4 cup grated Parmesan cheese
- 1/4 cup chopped fresh parsley
- 1 egg
- 2 cloves garlic, minced
- 1 teaspoon dried oregano
- 1/2 teaspoon dried basil
- Salt and black pepper to taste
- Olive oil for frying
- Marinara sauce, to serve
- Cooked spaghetti or rice, to serve

Method of Preparation

1. In a large bowl, combine the ground beef, ground lamb, breadcrumbs, grated Parmesan cheese, chopped fresh parsley, egg, minced garlic, dried oregano, dried basil, salt, and black pepper.
2. Mix the ingredients until well combined.
3. Form meat mixture into meatballs.

4. Heat the olive oil in a skillet over medium-high heat.
5. Add the meatballs and cook for about 10-12 minutes, turning to brown on all sides until cooked through.
6. Serve Italian Mediterranean Meatballs with marinara sauce and your choice of cooked spaghetti or rice.

Nutritional information (per serving, excluding sauce and garnish): Calories: 350 | Protein: 30g | Carbohydrates: 10g | Fat: 20g | Fiber: 1g

15. Greek-style grilled steak

Introduction: Greek-style grilled steak is a succulent and flavorful meat dish marinated with Mediterranean spices and herbs, usually served with a side of Greek salad.

Prep time: 15 minutes | Cook time: 10 minutes | Yield: 4 servings

Ingredients:

- 4 boneless ribeye or sirloin steaks
- 1/4 cup extra virgin olive oil
- 2 cloves garlic, minced
- 1 tablespoon chopped fresh rosemary
- 1 tablespoon chopped fresh thyme
- 1 teaspoon dried oregano
- Salt and black pepper to taste
- Lemon wedges, to decorate
- Greek salad, to serve

Method of Preparation

1. In a bowl, combine extra virgin olive oil, minced garlic, minced fresh rosemary, minced fresh thyme, dried oregano, salt, and black pepper.

2. Rub the fillets with the prepared mixture of herbs and spices.
3. Preheat a grill to medium-high heat.
4. Grill steaks for about 4 to 5 minutes per side over medium heat, or adjust cooking time to desired doneness.
5. Remove from the grill and let rest for a few minutes before serving.
6. Garnish with lemon slices.
7. Serve Greek-style grilled steak with Greek salad.

Nutritional information (per serving, excluding salad): Calories: 400 | Protein: 30g | Carbohydrates: 0g | Fat: 30g | Fiber: 0g

MEDITERRANEAN FISH AND SEAFOOD RECIPES

1. Baked Greek cod with lemon and herbs

Introduction: Baked Greek Cod with Lemon and Herbs is a light and flavorful dish featuring baked cod fillets with a Mediterranean-inspired lemon and herb sauce.

Prep time: 10 minutes | Cook time: 20 minutes | Yield: 4 servings

Ingredients:

- 4 cod fillets
- 1/4 cup extra virgin olive oil
- Juice of 1 lemon
- 2 cloves garlic, minced
- 1 teaspoon dried oregano
- 1 teaspoon dried thyme
- Salt and black pepper to taste
- Fresh parsley, to decorate (optional)
- Lemon slices, to decorate (optional)

Method of Preparation

1. Preheat your oven to 375°F (190°C).
2. In a bowl, combine the extra virgin olive oil, lemon juice, minced garlic, dried oregano, dried thyme, salt, and black pepper.
3. Place the cod fillets in a baking dish and pour the lemon and herb sauce on top.
4. Bake in the preheated oven for about 15-20 minutes, or until the cod is cooked through and flakes easily with a fork.
5. Garnish with fresh parsley and lemon wedges before serving.

Nutritional information (per serving): Calories: 200 | Protein: 25g | Carbohydrates: 2g | Fat: 10g | Fiber: 0g

2. Prawns with Mediterranean garlic

Introduction: Mediterranean Garlic Prawns are a classic Mediterranean dish that includes succulent shrimp cooked in a garlic, lemon and white wine sauce, and usually served with pasta or crusty bread.

Preparation time: 15 minutes | Cooking time: 15 minutes | Yield: 4 servings

Ingredients:

- 1 pound large shrimp, peeled and deveined
- 4 tablespoons unsalted butter
- 4 cloves garlic, minced
- Juice of 1 lemon
- 1/4 cup white wine
- 1/4 cup chopped fresh parsley
- Salt and black pepper to taste
- Crushed red pepper flakes (optional, for heating)
- Cooked pasta or crusty bread, to serve

Method of Preparation

1. In a large skillet, melt butter over medium-high heat.
2. Add minced garlic and sauté for about 1 minute until fragrant.
3. Add the shrimp to the pan and cook for 2-3 minutes per side until they turn pink and opaque.
4. Add the lemon juice, white wine, chopped fresh parsley, salt, black pepper, and optionally crushed red pepper flakes.
5. Simmer for another 2-3 minutes.
6. Serve Mediterranean Garlic Prawns over cooked pasta or with crusty bread.

Nutritional information (per serving, excluding pasta or bread): Calories: 200 | Protein: 20g | Carbohydrates: 3g | Fat: 10g | Fiber: 0g

3. Grilled Mediterranean Salmon

Introduction: Grilled Mediterranean Salmon is a delicious and healthy dish that includes salmon fillets marinated in Mediterranean herbs and grilled to perfection.

Prep time: 15 minutes | Cook time: 10 minutes | Yield: 4 servings

Ingredients:

- 4 salmon fillets
- 1/4 cup extra virgin olive oil
- Juice of 1 lemon
- 2 cloves garlic, minced
- 1 teaspoon dried oregano
- 1 teaspoon dried rosemary
- Salt and black pepper to taste
- Lemon slices, to decorate (optional)
- Fresh dill, to decorate (optional)

Method of Preparation

1. Preheat your grill to medium-high heat.
2. In a bowl, combine the extra virgin olive oil, lemon juice, minced garlic, dried oregano, dried rosemary, salt, and black pepper.
3. Place the salmon fillets on a shallow plate and pour the marinade over them. Turn to coat salmon evenly. Cover and refrigerate for at least 30 minutes.
4. Lightly oil grill grates to prevent sticking.
5. Grill the marinated salmon fillets for about 4-5 minutes per side, or until cooked to your desired level of doneness.

6. Optionally, garnish with lemon wedges and fresh dill before serving.

Nutritional information (per serving): Calories: 300 | Protein: 25g | Carbohydrates: 2g | Fat: 20g | Fiber: 0g

4. Tunisian fish tagine

Introduction: Tunisian fish tagine is a tasty and aromatic North African dish that includes fish, tomatoes, olives and a blend of Tunisian spices, typically cooked in a traditional clay tagine.

Prep time: 20 minutes | Cook time: 40 minutes | Yield: 4 servings

Ingredients:

- 4 fish fillets (such as snapper or sea bass)
- 2 tablespoons olive oil
- 1 onion, finely chopped
- 2 cloves garlic, minced
- 1 teaspoon ground cumin
- 1 teaspoon ground coriander
- 1/2 teaspoon ground paprika
- 1/2 teaspoon ground cayenne pepper (adjust to taste)
- 1 can (14 ounces) diced tomatoes
- 1/2 cup green olives, pitted
- 2 tablespoons chopped fresh cilantro
- Salt and black pepper to taste
- Lemon slices, to decorate (optional)
- Couscous or cooked rice, to serve

Method of Preparation

1. In a large tagine or deep skillet, heat the olive oil over medium heat.
2. Add the finely chopped onion and sauté until softened, about 3 to 4 minutes.
3. Add the minced garlic and cook for another minute.

4. Add ground cumin, ground coriander, ground paprika, and ground cayenne pepper. Cook for 2-3 minutes until fragrant.
5. Place the fish fillets on top of the spiced onion mixture.
6. Pour the diced tomatoes and green olives over the fish.
7. Cover the tagine or pan and simmer for about 25 to 30 minutes, or until the fish is cooked through.
8. Garnish with fresh chopped cilantro and optionally serve with lemon wedges and couscous or cooked rice.

Nutritional information (per serving, excluding couscous or rice): Calories: 250 | Protein: 30g | Carbohydrates: 10g | Fat: 10g | Fiber: 3g

5. Greek Fisherman Stew

Introduction: Greek Fisherman's Stew, known as "Kakavia," is a hearty Mediterranean fish stew that includes a variety of fish and shellfish simmered in a flavorful tomato-based broth.

Prep time: 20 minutes | Cook time: 45 minutes | Yield: 6 servings

Ingredients:

- 1 pound mixed fish and seafood (such as cod, shrimp, mussels, and squid), cleaned and cut into pieces
- 1/4 cup extra virgin olive oil
- 1 chopped onion
- 2 cloves garlic, minced
- 1 can (14 ounces) diced tomatoes
- 1/4 cup tomato paste
- 1/4 cup dry white wine
- 1 teaspoon dried oregano

- 1 teaspoon dried thyme
- 1/2 teaspoon dried rosemary
- 1 bay leaf
- 4 cups of fish or seafood broth
- Salt and black pepper to taste
- Chopped fresh parsley, to decorate (optional)
- Crunchy bread, to serve

Method of Preparation

1. In a large pot, heat extra virgin olive oil over medium heat.
2. Add the chopped onion and sauté until softened, about 3 to 4 minutes.
3. Add the minced garlic and cook for another minute.
4. Add the diced tomatoes, tomato paste, dry white wine, dried oregano, dried thyme, dried rosemary and bay leaf. Cook for 5-7 minutes until mixture thickens.
5. Pour in the fish or seafood broth and bring to a simmer.
6. Add fish and seafood mixture to boiling broth.
7. Cover the pot and let it simmer for about 20-25 minutes, or until the fish and seafood are cooked through.
8. Season with salt and black pepper to taste.
9. Optionally, garnish with fresh chopped parsley before serving.
10. Serve Greek fisherman stew with crusty bread.

Nutritional information (per serving, excluding bread): Calories: 250 | Protein: 30g | Carbohydrates: 10g | Fat: 10g | Fiber: 3g

Introduction: Lemon Garlic Grilled Shrimp is a quick and easy Mediterranean dish that features succulent shrimp marinated in lemon garlic sauce and grilled to perfection.

Prep time: 15 minutes | Cook time: 5 minutes | Yield: 4 servings

Ingredients:

- 1 pound large shrimp, peeled and deveined
- 1/4 cup extra virgin olive oil
- Juice of 2 lemons
- 4 cloves garlic, minced
- 1 teaspoon dried oregano
- Salt and black pepper to taste
- Lemon slices, to decorate (optional)
- Chopped fresh parsley, to decorate (optional)

Method of Preparation

1. In a bowl, combine the extra virgin olive oil, lemon juice, minced garlic, dried oregano, salt, and black pepper.
2. Place the peeled and deveined shrimp on a shallow plate and pour the lemon-garlic marinade over them. Toss to coat. Cover and refrigerate for at least 30 minutes.
3. Preheat your grill to medium-high heat.
4. Thread the marinated shrimp onto skewers.
5. Grill the shrimp skewers for about 2-3 minutes per side, or until pink and opaque.
6. Optionally, garnish with lemon wedges and fresh chopped parsley before serving.

Nutritional information (per serving): Calories: 200 | Protein: 25g | Carbohydrates: 3g | Fat: 10g | Fiber: 0g

6. Grilled Shrimp with Lemon and Garlic

7. Mediterranean Italian sea bass

Introduction: Italian Mediterranean Sea Bass is a delicious dish that includes sea bass fillets cooked with Italian herbs, tomatoes, olives and capers.

Prep time: 15 minutes | Cook time: 25 minutes | Yield: 4 servings

Ingredients:

- 4 sea bass fillets
- 1/4 cup extra virgin olive oil
- 1 onion, finely chopped
- 2 cloves garlic, minced
- 1 can (14 ounces) diced tomatoes
- 1/4 cup green olives, pitted and sliced
- 2 tablespoons capers
- 1 teaspoon dried basil
- 1/2 teaspoon dried oregano
- Salt and black pepper to taste
- Lemon slices, to decorate (optional)
- Chopped fresh basil, to decorate (optional)

Method of Preparation

1. In a large skillet, heat the extra virgin olive oil over medium heat.
2. Add the finely chopped onion and sauté until softened, about 3 to 4 minutes.
3. Add the minced garlic and cook for another minute.
4. Add the diced tomatoes, green olives, capers, dried basil, dried oregano, salt and black pepper. Cook for 5-7 minutes until the mixture thickens slightly.
5. Place the sea bass fillets on top of the tomato mixture in the pan.
6. Cover the pan and let it simmer for about 15-20 minutes, or until the sea bass is cooked through.

7. Optionally, garnish with lemon wedges and chopped fresh basil before serving.

Nutritional information (per serving): Calories: 250 | Protein: 30g | Carbohydrates: 10g | Fat: 10g | Fiber: 3g

8. Spiced Grilled Moroccan Swordfish

Introduction: Grilled Swordfish with Moroccan Spices is a tasty dish that includes swordfish fillets marinated in Moroccan spices and grilled to perfection.

Prep time: 20 minutes | Cook time: 10 minutes | Yield: 4 servings

Ingredients:

- 4 swordfish fillets
- 1/4 cup extra virgin olive oil
- Juice of 1 lemon
- 2 teaspoons ground cumin
- 1 teaspoon ground coriander
- 1 teaspoon ground paprika
- 1/2 teaspoon ground cinnamon
- 1/4 teaspoon ground cayenne pepper (adjust to taste)
- Salt and black pepper to taste
- Lemon slices, to decorate (optional)
- Fresh cilantro, to decorate (optional)

Method of Preparation

1. In a bowl, combine the extra virgin olive oil, lemon juice, ground cumin, ground coriander, ground paprika, ground cinnamon, ground cayenne pepper, salt, and black pepper.

2. Place the swordfish fillets on a shallow plate and pour the Moroccan spice marinade over them. Turn to coat. Cover and refrigerate for at least 30 minutes.
3. Preheat your grill to medium-high heat.
4. Grill the marinated swordfish fillets for about 4-5 minutes per side, or until cooked to your desired level of doneness.
5. Optionally, garnish with lime wedges and fresh cilantro before serving.

Nutritional information (per serving): Calories: 300 | Protein: 30g | Carbohydrates: 2g | | Fat: 20g | Fiber: 0g

9. Mediterranean tuna salad

Introduction: Mediterranean tuna salad is a refreshing and healthy salad that contains flaky tuna, vegetables, olives and feta cheese, dressed with a lemon and oregano vinaigrette.

Prep time: 15 minutes | Cook time: 0 minutes | Yield: 4 servings

Ingredients:

- 2 cans (5 ounces each) tuna, drained
- 1 cup cherry tomatoes, cut in half
- 1/2 cucumber, diced
- 1/4 red onion, thinly sliced
- 1/4 cup Kalamata olives, pitted and sliced
- 1/4 cup crumbled feta cheese
- 2 tablespoons chopped fresh parsley
- Juice of 1 lemon
- 2 tablespoons extra virgin olive oil
- 1 teaspoon dried oregano
- Salt and black pepper to taste
- Romaine lettuce leaves, to serve (optional)
- Crispy bread, to serve (optional)

Method of Preparation

1. In a large bowl, combine the drained tuna, halved cherry tomatoes, diced cucumber, thinly sliced red onion, Kalamata olives, crumbled feta cheese, and chopped fresh parsley.
2. In a small bowl, whisk together the lemon juice, extra virgin olive oil, dried oregano, salt, and black pepper to make the vinaigrette.
3. Pour the vinaigrette over the tuna salad and toss to coat.
4. Optionally, serve the Mediterranean Tuna Salad on a bed of romaine lettuce leaves or with crusty bread.

Nutritional information (per serving, excluding lettuce or bread): Calories: 250 | Protein: 25g | Carbohydrates: 6g | Fat: 15g | Fiber: 2g

10. Greek Stuffed Squid

Introduction: Greek stuffed squid is a delicious Mediterranean dish that features tender squid stuffed with a flavorful blend of rice, herbs and spices, then simmered in a tomato-based sauce.

Prep time: 30 minutes | Cook time: 45 minutes | Yield: 4 servings

Ingredients:

- 8 small to medium sized squid, cleaned and tentacles reserved
- 1/2 cup arborio rice
- 1/4 cup chopped fresh parsley
- 1/4 cup chopped fresh mint
- 1/4 cup chopped fresh dill
- 1 onion, finely chopped

- 2 cloves garlic, minced
- 1/4 cup extra virgin olive oil
- 1 can (14 ounces) diced tomatoes
- 1/2 teaspoon ground cinnamon
- Salt and black pepper to taste
- Lemon slices, to decorate (optional)

Method of Preparation

1. Rinse the cleaned squid under cold water and pat dry with paper towels.
2. In a large bowl, combine Arborio rice, chopped fresh parsley, chopped fresh mint, chopped fresh dill, finely chopped onion, minced garlic, extra virgin olive oil, ground cinnamon, salt and pepper black.
3. Fill each squid tube with the rice and herb mixture, leaving some room at the top for it to expand. Secure openings with toothpicks.
4. In a deep skillet, heat extra virgin olive oil over medium heat.
5. Add the stuffed squid and reserved tentacles to the pan. Sauté for about 5 minutes until lightly browned.
6. Pour the diced tomatoes over the squid and add enough water to cover.
7. Cover the pan and let it simmer for about 30-35 minutes, or until the rice is cooked and the squid is tender.
8. Optionally, garnish with lemon slices before serving.

Nutritional information (per serving, excluding optional garnish): Calories: 300 | Protein: 25g | Carbohydrates: 30g | Fat: 10g | Fiber: 3g

11. Spanish seafood paella

Introduction: Spanish Seafood Paella is a classic Mediterranean rice dish featuring a vibrant combination of seafood, saffron-infused rice, and a variety of aromatic spices.

Prep time: 20 minutes | Cook time: 40 minutes | Yield: 6 servings

Ingredients:

- 1 cup arborio rice
- 12 large shrimp, peeled and deveined
- 1/2 pound mussels, cleaned and trimmed
- 1/2 pound clams, washed
- 1/2 pound squid rings
- 1 onion, finely chopped
- 1 red bell pepper, thinly sliced
- 1 yellow bell pepper, thinly sliced
- 4 cloves garlic, minced
- 1/4 cup extra virgin olive oil
- 1/4 teaspoon saffron threads, soaked in 1/4 cup warm water
- 1 teaspoon smoked paprika
- 1 teaspoon ground turmeric
- 1/2 teaspoon paprika
- Salt and black pepper to taste
- Lemon slices, to decorate (optional)
- Chopped fresh parsley, to decorate (optional)

Method of Preparation

1. In a large paella pan or deep frying pan, heat extra virgin olive oil over medium heat.
2. Add the finely chopped onion and sauté until softened, about 3 to 4 minutes.
3. Add the thinly sliced red and yellow peppers and minced garlic. Cook for a further 3-4 minutes until the peppers soften.
4. Add Arborio rice, smoked paprika, ground turmeric, paprika and saffron-infused water. Stir to coat the rice with the spices.
5. Place the seafood (shrimp, mussels, clams, and squid) on top of the rice mixture.
6. Pour enough water into the pan to cover the rice and seafood.

7. Cover the pan and simmer for about 20-25 minutes, or until the rice is cooked, the seafood is tender, and the liquid is absorbed.
8. Season with salt and black pepper to taste.
9. Optionally, garnish with lemon wedges and fresh chopped parsley before serving.

Nutritional information (per serving, excluding optional garnish): Calories: 350 | Protein: 25g | Carbohydrates: 30g | Fat: 15g | Fiber: 2g

12. Baked Mediterranean Tilapia

Introduction: Baked Mediterranean tilapia is a simple but tasty dish that includes tilapia fillets baked with tomatoes, olives, capers and Mediterranean herbs.

Prep time: 15 minutes | Cooking time: 20 minutes | Yield: 4 servings

Ingredients:

- 4 tilapia fillets
- 1 can (14 ounces) diced tomatoes
- 1/4 cup Kalamata olives, pitted and sliced
- 2 tablespoons capers
- 2 cloves garlic, minced
- 1 teaspoon dried oregano
- 1/2 teaspoon dried basil
- 1/2 teaspoon dried thyme
- 1/4 teaspoon crushed red pepper flakes (adjust to taste)
- Salt and black pepper to taste
- Lemon slices, to decorate (optional)
- Chopped fresh parsley, to decorate (optional)

Method of Preparation

1. Preheat your oven to 375°F (190°C).
2. In a baking dish, combine the diced tomatoes, sliced Kalamata olives, capers, minced garlic, dried oregano, dried basil, dried thyme, crushed red pepper flakes, salt and pepper black.
3. Place tilapia fillets on top of tomato mixture in baking dish.
4. Cover the dish with aluminum foil and bake in the preheated oven for about 15 minutes.
5. Remove foil and bake for 5 to 7 minutes more, or until tilapia is cooked through and flakes easily with a fork.
6. Optionally, garnish with lemon wedges and fresh chopped parsley before serving.

Nutritional information (per serving, excluding optional garnish): Calories: 200 | Protein: 25g | Carbohydrates: 6g | Fat: 8g | Fiber: 2g

13. Grilled Sicilian sardines

Introduction: Grilled Sicilian sardines are a traditional Mediterranean dish that includes fresh sardines marinated with Sicilian flavors and grilled to perfection.

Prep time: 20 minutes | Cooking time: 10 minutes | Yield: 4 servings

Ingredients:

- 12 fresh sardines, cleaned and gutted
- 1/4 cup extra virgin olive oil
- Juice of 1 lemon
- 2 cloves garlic, minced
- 1/4 cup chopped fresh parsley
- 1/4 teaspoon dried oregano
- Salt and black pepper to taste
- Lemon slices, to decorate (optional)

Method of Preparation

1. Preheat your grill to medium-high heat.
2. In a bowl, combine the extra virgin olive oil, lemon juice, minced garlic, minced fresh parsley, dried oregano, salt, and black pepper.
3. Place the cleaned and gutted sardines on a shallow plate and pour the marinade over them. Turn to coat. Cover and refrigerate for at least 30 minutes.
4. Lightly oil grill grates to prevent sticking.
5. Grill the marinated sardines for about 2-3 minutes per side, or until cooked through and have grill marks.
6. Optionally, garnish with lemon wedges before serving.

Nutritional information (per serving, excluding optional garnish): Calories: 200 | Protein: 20g | Carbohydrates: 0g | Fat: 15g | Fiber: 0g

14. Grilled Turkish Octopus

Introduction: Grilled Turkish Octopus is a Mediterranean delicacy featuring tender octopus marinated in Turkish spices and grilled to perfection.

Prep time: 20 minutes | Cooking time: 15 minutes | Yield: 4 servings

Ingredients:

- 2 octopuses, clean and with tentacles separated
- 1/4 cup extra virgin olive oil
- Juice of 1 lemon
- 2 cloves garlic, minced
- 1 teaspoon ground cumin
- 1/2 teaspoon ground paprika

- 1/4 teaspoon crushed red pepper flakes (adjust to taste)
- Salt and black pepper to taste
- Lemon slices, to decorate (optional)
- Chopped fresh parsley, to decorate (optional)

Method of Preparation

1. In a bowl, combine the extra virgin olive oil, lemon juice, minced garlic, ground cumin, ground paprika, crushed red pepper flakes, salt, and black pepper.
2. Place the clean octopus and tentacles on a shallow plate and pour the marinade over them. Turn to coat. Cover and refrigerate for at least 30 minutes.
3. Preheat your grill to medium-high heat.
4. Grill the marinated octopus and tentacles for about 2-3 minutes per side, or until they have grill marks and are cooked through.
5. Optionally, garnish with lemon wedges and fresh chopped parsley before serving.

Nutritional information (per serving, excluding optional garnish): Calories: 250 | Protein: 30g | Carbohydrates: 2g | Fat: 15g | Fiber: 0g

15. Moroccan fish and chickpea tagine

Introduction: Moroccan Fish and Chickpea Tagine is a fragrant and hearty dish featuring fish, chickpeas and a blend of Moroccan spices, usually cooked in a traditional clay tagine.

Preparation time: 20 minutes | Cooking time: 40 minutes | Yield: 4 servings

Ingredients:

- 4 fish fillets (such as tilapia or cod)
- 1 can (14 ounces) chickpeas, drained and rinsed
- 1 onion, finely chopped
- 2 cloves garlic, minced
- 1/4 cup extra virgin olive oil
- 1 teaspoon ground cumin
- 1 teaspoon ground coriander
- 1 teaspoon ground paprika
- 1/2 teaspoon ground cinnamon
- 1/4 teaspoon ground cayenne pepper (adjust to taste)
- 1 can (14 ounces) diced tomatoes
- 1/4 cup chopped fresh cilantro
- Salt and black pepper to taste
- Lemon slices, to decorate (optional)
- Cooked couscous, to serve

Method of Preparation

1. In a large tagine or deep skillet, heat the extra virgin olive oil over medium heat.

2. Add the finely chopped onion and sauté until softened, about 3 to 4 minutes.

3. Add the minced garlic and cook for another minute.

4. Add ground cumin, ground coriander, ground paprika, ground cinnamon, and ground cayenne pepper. Cook for 2-3 minutes until fragrant.

5. Place the fish fillets on top of the spiced onion mixture.

6. Pour the diced tomatoes and chickpeas over the fish.

7. Cover the tagine or pan and simmer for about 20-25 minutes, or until the fish is cooked through.

8. Garnish with fresh chopped cilantro.

9. Serve the Moroccan Fish and Chickpea Tagine with lemon wedges and cooked couscous.

Nutritional information (per serving, excluding couscous): Calories: 300 | Protein: 30g | Carbohydrates: 10g | Fat: 15g | Fiber: 3g

MEDITERRANEAN SAUCES, DIPS, DRESSINGS

1. Tzatziki Sauce

Introduction: Tzatziki sauce is a classic Greek condiment made with yogurt, cucumbers, and fresh herbs. It is a refreshing and creamy sauce or dip that combines perfectly with a wide range of Mediterranean dishes.

Prep time: 10 minutes | Cooking time: 0 minutes | Yield: Approximately 1 cup

Ingredients:

- 1 cup Greek yogurt
- 1 cucumber, grated and drained
- 2 cloves garlic, minced
- 1 tablespoon extra virgin olive oil
- 1 tablespoon fresh lemon juice
- 1 tablespoon fresh dill, chopped
- Salt and black pepper to taste

Method of Preparation

1. In a bowl, combine the Greek yogurt, grated and drained cucumber, minced garlic, extra virgin olive oil, fresh lemon juice, and chopped fresh dill.
2. Season with salt and black pepper to taste.
3. Mix all ingredients until well combined.
4. Refrigerate for at least 30 minutes to allow the flavors to blend before serving.

Nutritional information (per 2 tablespoon serving): Calories: 30 | Protein: 2g | Carbohydrates: 2g | Fat: 2g | Fiber: 0g

2. Hummus

Introduction: Hummus is a popular Middle Eastern dip made with creamy chickpeas, tahini, and aromatic spices. It's a versatile dip or dip that's perfect for pita bread, vegetables, or as a condiment.

Preparation time: 10 minutes | Cooking time: 0 minutes | Yield: approximately 2 cups

Ingredients:

- 1 can (15 ounces) chickpeas, drained and rinsed
- 1/4 cup tahini
- 2 cloves garlic, minced
- 2 tablespoons extra virgin olive oil
- Juice of 1 lemon
- 1 teaspoon ground cumin
- Salt and black pepper to taste
- Water, as needed
- Paprika and extra olive oil, to decorate (optional)

Method of Preparation

1. In a food processor, combine the chickpeas, tahini, minced garlic, extra virgin olive oil, lemon juice, ground cumin, salt, and black pepper.
2. Process the mixture until it forms a smooth, creamy paste. If it is too thick, you can add water little by little until you reach the desired consistency.
3. Transfer hummus to a serving platter.
4. Optionally, garnish with a pinch of paprika and an extra drizzle of olive oil before serving.

Nutritional information (per 2 tablespoon serving): Calories: 50 | Protein: 2g | Carbohydrates: 5g | Fat: 3g | Fiber: 2g

3. Baba Ganush

Introduction: Baba Ganoush is a creamy, smoky Middle Eastern dip made with roasted eggplant, tahini, and a mix of flavorful ingredients. It is a perfect accompaniment to pita bread or as a sauce for vegetables.

Prep time: 15 minutes | Cook time: 25 minutes (to roast the eggplant) | Yield: approximately 2 cups

Ingredients:

- 2 medium eggplants
- 1/4 cup tahini
- 2 cloves garlic, minced
- Juice of 1 lemon
- 2 tablespoons extra virgin olive oil
- 1 teaspoon ground cumin
- Salt and black pepper to taste
- Chopped fresh parsley and extra olive oil, to decorate (optional)

Method of Preparation

1. Preheat your oven to 400°F (200°C).
2. Prick the eggplants with a fork and place them on a baking sheet. Roast them in the preheated oven for about 25 minutes, or until they are soft and the skin is charred.
3. Remove the eggplants from the oven and let them cool.
4. Once cooled, peel the eggplants and place the pulp in a bowl.
5. In the same bowl, add the tahini, minced garlic, lemon juice, extra virgin olive oil, ground cumin, salt, and black pepper.
6. Blend and mix all the ingredients until you achieve a smooth and creamy consistency.
7. Transfer the Baba Ganoush to a serving platter.
8. Optionally, garnish with fresh chopped parsley and a drizzle of olive oil before serving.

Nutritional information (per 2 tablespoon serving): Calories: 40 | Protein: 1g | Carbohydrates: 4g | Fat: 3g | Fiber: 2g

4. Greek Salad Dressing

Introduction: Greek Salad Dressing is a spicy, herb-infused vinaigrette that adds flavor to any salad. It's the perfect dressing to enhance your Greek salad or other fresh green salads.

Prep time: 5 minutes | Cook time: 0 minutes | Yield: Approximately 1 cup

Ingredients:

- 1/2 cup extra virgin olive oil
- 1/4 cup red wine vinegar
- 1 clove garlic, minced
- 1 teaspoon Dijon mustard
- 1 teaspoon dried oregano
- Salt and black pepper to taste

Method of Preparation

1. In a bowl, whisk together the extra virgin olive oil, red wine vinegar, minced garlic, Dijon mustard, dried oregano, salt and black pepper.
2. Continue whisking until dressing is emulsified.
3. Store Greek salad dressing in an airtight container in the refrigerator. Shake or shake before use.

Nutritional information (per 2 tablespoon serving): Calories: 120 | Protein: 0g | Carbohydrates: 0g | Fat: 14g | Fiber: 0g

5. Tahini Sauce

Introduction: Tahini sauce is a creamy, nutty condiment made from sesame paste. It is a versatile sauce used in several Mediterranean and Middle Eastern dishes, such as falafel and shawarma.

Prep time: 5 minutes | Cooking time: 0 minutes | Yield: Approximately 1 cup

Ingredients:

- 1/2 cup tahini
- 2 cloves garlic, minced
- Juice of 1 lemon
- 2 tablespoons extra virgin olive oil
- Water, as needed
- Salt and black pepper to taste
- Chopped fresh parsley, to decorate (optional)

Method of Preparation

1. In a bowl, combine the tahini, minced garlic, lemon juice, extra virgin olive oil, salt, and black pepper.
2. Mix the ingredients. The mixture will become thick.
3. Gradually add water, a little at a time, and continue mixing until the sauce reaches the desired consistency. It should be smooth and creamy.
4. Optionally, garnish with fresh chopped parsley before serving.

Nutritional information (per 2 tablespoon serving): Calories: 60 | Protein: 1g | Carbohydrates: 2g | Fat: 6g | Fiber: 1g

6. Mediterranean Sauce

Introduction: Mediterranean sauce is a fresh and vibrant condiment filled with diced tomatoes, cucumbers, red onion and aromatic herbs. It's a delicious topping for grilled meats or a topping for pita chips.

Prep time: 10 minutes | Cooking time: 0 minutes | Yield: approximately 2 cups

Ingredients:

- 2 tomatoes, diced
- 1 cucumber, diced
- 1/2 red onion, finely chopped
- 1/4 cup fresh parsley, chopped
- 1/4 cup fresh mint, chopped
- Juice of 1 lemon
- 2 tablespoons extra virgin olive oil
- Salt and black pepper to taste

Method of Preparation

1. In a bowl, combine the diced tomatoes, diced cucumber, finely chopped red onion, chopped fresh parsley, and chopped fresh mint.
2. Add the juice of one lemon and the extra virgin olive oil.
3. Season with salt and black pepper to taste.
4. Mix all ingredients until well combined.
5. Refrigerate for at least 30 minutes to allow the flavors to blend before serving.

Nutritional information (per 1/2 cup serving): Calories: 30 | Protein: 1g | Carbohydrates: 4g | Fat: 1g | Fiber: 1g

7. Harissa Sauce

Introduction: Harissa sauce is a spicy and aromatic North African condiment made with chili peppers, garlic and a blend of flavorful spices. Adds a spicy touch to various dishes.

Prep time: 10 minutes | Cooking time: 5 minutes | Yield: Approximately 1 cup

Ingredients:

- 8 dried red chilies, soaked in hot water and seeded
- 2 cloves of garlic
- 2 tablespoons extra virgin olive oil
- 1 teaspoon ground cumin
- 1 teaspoon ground coriander
- 1/2 teaspoon ground caraway seeds
- 1/2 teaspoon smoked paprika
- Salt to taste

Method of Preparation

1. In a food processor, combine the soaked and seeded dried red chile peppers, garlic, extra virgin olive oil, ground cumin, ground coriander, ground caraway seeds, smoked paprika, and salt.
2. Blend the ingredients until a smooth paste forms. You may need to scrape the sides of the food processor bowl several times.
3. Transfer the Harissa sauce to an airtight container. It can be refrigerated for several weeks.

Nutritional information (per 2 tablespoon serving): Calories: 20 | Protein: 0g | Carbohydrates: 2g | Fat: 2g | Fiber: 0g

8. Greek Taramasalata

Introduction: Greek taramasalata is a creamy, salty sauce made with fish roe, olive oil, and lemon juice. It is a classic Greek appetizer that is often enjoyed with pita bread.

Prep time: 10 minutes | Cook time: 0 minutes | Yield: Approximately 1 cup

Ingredients:

- 1/2 cup fish roe (usually carp or cod)
- 1/2 cup extra virgin olive oil
- Juice of 1 lemon
- 1 small onion, grated
- 2 cloves garlic, minced
- White bread, without crust and soaked in water.
- Salt and black pepper to taste

Method of Preparation

1. In a food processor, combine the fish roe, extra virgin olive oil, juice of one lemon, grated onion, minced garlic and soaked white bread.
2. Blend the ingredients until they form a smooth and creamy consistency.
3. Season with salt and black pepper to taste.
4. Refrigerate for at least 30 minutes before serving.

Nutritional information (per 2 tablespoon serving): Calories: 100 | Protein: 2g | Carbohydrates: 2g | Fat: 10g | Fiber: 0g

9. Romesco Sauce

Introduction: Romesco sauce is a rich, nutty Spanish condiment made with roasted red peppers, tomatoes, almonds, and a blend of spices. It is a versatile sauce that is used in several Mediterranean dishes.

Preparation time: 15 minutes | Cooking time: 15 minutes (for roasting) | Yield: approximately 2 cups

Ingredients:

- 2 red peppers, roasted, peeled and seeded
- 1 roasted tomato
- 1/2 cup toasted almonds
- 2 cloves garlic, minced
- 2 tablespoons extra virgin olive oil
- 1 tablespoon red wine vinegar
- 1 teaspoon smoked paprika
- 1/2 teaspoon ground cayenne pepper (adjust to taste)
- Salt and black pepper to taste

Method of Preparation

1. Roast the red peppers and tomato until charred and tender. Once cooled, peel and seed the peppers.
2. In a food processor, combine the roasted red peppers, roasted tomato, toasted almonds, minced garlic, extra virgin olive oil, red wine vinegar, smoked paprika, ground cayenne pepper, salt and black pepper.
3. Blend the ingredients until a smooth sauce is formed.
4. Taste and adjust seasonings as needed.
5. Refrigerate Romesco sauce for at least 30 minutes before using.

Nutritional information (per 2 tablespoon serving): Calories: 60 | Protein: 2g | Carbohydrates: 3g | Fat: 5g | Fiber: 1g

10. Avgolemono Greek Sauce

Introduction: Avgolemono Greek Sauce is a velvety, tangy sauce made from a mixture of eggs and lemon juice. It is often used to add creaminess and flavor to soups and Mediterranean dishes.

Preparation time: 10 minutes | Cooking time: 10 minutes | Yield: Approximately 1 cup

Ingredients:

- 2 large eggs
- Juice of 2 lemons
- 1 cup chicken broth
- 2 tablespoons cornstarch
- Salt and black pepper to taste

Method of Preparation

1. In a bowl, whisk together the eggs and lemon juice until well combined.
2. In a saucepan, heat chicken broth over medium heat until simmering.
3. In a separate small bowl, dissolve the cornstarch in a small amount of water to create a slurry.
4. Slowly pour the egg and lemon mixture into the boiling broth while whisking continuously.
5. Add the cornstarch mixture to the mixture and continue whisking until the sauce thickens.
6. Season with salt and black pepper to taste.
7. Remove from heat and let cool slightly before using.

Nutritional information (per 2 tablespoon serving): Calories: 30 | Protein: 1g | Carbohydrates: 2g | Fat: 2g | Fiber: 0g

11. Mediterranean pesto

Introduction: Mediterranean pesto is a flavorful variation on traditional pesto that includes ingredients such as sun-dried tomatoes, Kalamata olives, and fresh basil. It is a versatile sauce that can be used with pasta, sandwiches, or as a dip.

Prep time: 10 minutes | Cooking time: 0 minutes | Yield: Approximately 1 cup

Ingredients:

- 1 cup fresh basil leaves
- 1/2 cup sun-dried tomatoes (packed in oil), drained
- 1/4 cup Kalamata olives, pitted
- 1/4 cup grated Parmesan cheese
- 2 cloves of garlic
- 1/4 cup extra virgin olive oil
- Juice of 1 lemon
- Salt and black pepper to taste

Method of Preparation

1. In a food processor, combine fresh basil leaves, sun-dried tomatoes, pitted Kalamata olives, grated Parmesan cheese, garlic cloves, extra virgin olive oil, and juice of one lemon.
2. Blend the ingredients until you achieve a smooth pesto sauce.
3. Season with salt and black pepper to taste.
4. Refrigerate for at least 30 minutes before serving.

Nutritional information (per 2 tablespoon serving): Calories: 60 | Protein: 1g | Carbohydrates: 2g | Fat: 6g | Fiber: 1g

12. Moroccan Chermoula Sauce

Introduction: Moroccan Chermoula sauce is a spicy, herbaceous sauce used in North African cuisine. It's made with a blend of fresh herbs, spices and citrus, making it perfect for marinating meats or as a sauce.

Prep time: 10 minutes | Cooking time: 0 minutes | Yield: Approximately 1 cup

Ingredients:

- 1 cup fresh cilantro, chopped
- 1 cup fresh parsley, chopped

- 3 cloves garlic, minced
- Juice of 1 lemon
- 2 teaspoons ground cumin
- 1 teaspoon ground coriander
- 1/2 teaspoon ground paprika
- 1/4 teaspoon ground cayenne pepper (adjust to taste)
- 1/4 cup extra virgin olive oil
- Salt and black pepper to taste

Method of Preparation

1. In a food processor, combine fresh cilantro, fresh parsley, minced garlic, juice of one lemon, ground cumin, ground coriander, ground paprika, ground cayenne pepper, extra virgin olive oil, salt and black pepper.
2. Blend the ingredients until they form a smooth and vibrant sauce.
3. Taste and adjust seasonings as needed.
4. Refrigerate for at least 30 minutes before using.

Nutritional information (per 2 tablespoon serving): Calories: 30 | Protein: 0g | Carbohydrates: 2g | Fat: 3g | Fiber: 1g

13. Labneh Sauce

Introduction: Labneh Dip is a creamy, tangy Middle Eastern dip made with strained yogurt. It is often served with pita bread or as a dip for vegetables.

Prep time: 10 minutes | Cook time: 0 minutes | Yield: Approximately 1 cup

Ingredients:

- 1 cup labneh (strained yogurt)

- 1 clove garlic, minced
- 2 tablespoons extra virgin olive oil
- 1 teaspoon dried mint
- Salt and black pepper to taste

Preparation method:

1. In a bowl, combine the labneh, minced garlic, extra virgin olive oil, dried mint, salt, and black pepper.
2. Mix all ingredients until well combined.
3. Refrigerate for at least 30 minutes before serving.

Nutritional information (per 2 tablespoon serving): Calories: 40 | Protein: 2g | Carbohydrates: 1g | Fat: 4g | Fiber: 0g

14. Olive tapenada

Introduction: Olive tapenade is a salty, savory Mediterranean condiment made with a blend of olives, capers, and aromatic herbs. It is a versatile dipping or dipping sauce.

Preparation time: 10 minutes | Cooking time: 0 minutes | Yield: Approximately 1 cup

Ingredients:

- 1 cup Kalamata olives, pitted
- 2 tablespoons capers, drained
- 2 cloves garlic, minced
- 2 tablespoons fresh parsley, chopped
- 1 teaspoon fresh thyme leaves
- Juice of 1 lemon
- 2 tablespoons extra virgin olive oil
- Salt and black pepper to taste

Method of Preparation

1. In a food processor, combine pitted Kalamata olives, capers, minced garlic,

fresh parsley, fresh thyme leaves, juice of one lemon, extra virgin olive oil, salt and black pepper.

2. Pulse the ingredients until they form a thick paste with some texture.
3. Taste and adjust seasonings as needed.
4. Refrigerate for at least 30 minutes before serving.

Nutritional information (per 2 tablespoon serving): Calories: 30 | Protein: 0g | Carbohydrates: 2g | Fat: 3g | Fiber: 1g

15. Mediterranean Red Pepper Sauce

Introduction: Mediterranean Red Pepper Sauce is a vibrant and flavorful condiment made with roasted red peppers and a blend of Mediterranean spices. Adds a burst of color and flavor to various dishes.

Preparation time: 15 minutes | Cooking time: 15 minutes (for roasting) | Yield: Approximately 1 cup

Ingredients:

- 2 red peppers, roasted, peeled and seeded
- 2 cloves garlic, minced
- 1/4 cup extra virgin olive oil
- Juice of 1 lemon
- 1 teaspoon ground cumin
- 1/2 teaspoon ground cilantro
- 1/4 teaspoon smoked paprika
- Salt and black pepper to taste

Method of Preparation

1. Roast red peppers until charred and tender. Once cooled, peel and seed the peppers.
2. In a food processor, combine the roasted red peppers, minced garlic, extra virgin olive oil, juice of one lemon, ground cumin, ground coriander, smoked paprika, salt and black pepper.
3. Blend the ingredients until a smooth sauce is formed.
4. Taste and adjust seasonings as needed.
5. Refrigerate for at least 30 minutes before using.

Nutritional information (per 2 tablespoon serving): Calories: 50 | Protein: 0g | Carbohydrates: 3g | Fat: 5g | Fiber: 1g

RECIPES INDEX

60 DAYS MEAL PLAN

DAY	BREAKFAST	LUNCH	DINNER	DESSERT
1	Mediterranean Breakfast Bowl	Greek Gyro Sandwich + Greek Salad	Greek Chicken Souvlaki + Roasted Mediterranean Vegetables	Greek Yogurt Parfait
2	Shakshuka	Mediterranean Quinoa Salad + Tzatziki Sauce	Baked Greek Cod with Lemon and Herbs + Mediterranean Rice Pilaf	Labneh with Honey and Pistachios
3	Greek Oatmeal with Honey and Walnuts	Mediterranean Vegetarian Wrap + Hummus	Moroccan Chicken Tagine + Greek Lemon Roasted Potatoes	Mediterranean Breakfast Burrito
4	Turkish Menemen	Greek Lentil Soup + Mediterranean Couscous Salad	Grilled Mediterranean Lamb Chops + Stuffed Grape Leaves (Dolmas)	Mediterranean Scrambled Eggs (made sweet with honey and nuts)
5	Mediterranean Avocado Toast	Mediterranean Chickpea Stew + Tabuli Salad	Spanish Chicken and Chorizo Paella + Roasted Garlic Tomato Bruschetta	Spanakopita Breakfast Casserole (made sweet, if possible)
6	Breakfast Frittata with Olives and Tomato	Mediterranean Rice and Beans + Greek Roast Potatoes	Grilled Mediterranean Salmon + Greek-style Green Beans	Mediterranean Breakfast Wrap (with a sweet twist)
7	Mediterranean Scrambled Eggs	Mediterranean White Bean Salad + Baba Ganush	Greek Lemon Garlic Chicken + Mediterranean Zucchini Fritters	Greek Yogurt Parfait
8	Breakfast Quesadilla with Feta and Spinach	Mediterranean Bulgur Salad + Greek Salad	Prawns with Mediterranean Garlic + Roasted Beet Salad with Feta Cheese	Labneh with Honey and Pistachios

9	Spanakopita Breakfast Casserole	Mediterranean Tuna Wrap + Marinated Olives	Greek Moussaka + Greek-style Green Beans	Greek Yogurt Parfait
10	Mediterranean Omelet	Lebanese Mujadara + Greek Roast Potatoes	Moroccan Lamb Stew + Mediterranean Roasted Red Peppers	Mediterranean Breakfast Burrito (with a sweet twist)
11	Mediterranean Scrambled Eggs	Mediterranean Couscous with Chickpeas + Tabuli Salad	Baked Mediterranean Tilapia + Greek Lemon Roasted Potatoes	Labneh with Honey and Pistachios
12	Quinoa for Mediterranean Breakfast	Mediterranean Vegetarian Quesadilla + Hummus	Mediterranean Pork Souvlaki + Roasted Mediterranean Vegetables	Greek Yogurt Parfait
13	Greek Oatmeal with Honey and Walnuts	Greek Chicken Pita Souvlaki + Mediterranean Chickpea Salad	Grilled Shrimp with Lemon and Garlic + Tomato and Cucumber Salad	Mediterranean Breakfast Wrap (with a sweet twist)
14	Mediterranean Avocado Toast	Mediterranean Rice Pilaf + Greek Salad	Grilled Turkish Octopus + Mediterranean Zucchini Fritters	Labneh with Honey and Pistachios
15	Breakfast Frittata with Olives and Tomato	Mediterranean White Bean Salad + Baba Ganush	Grilled Mediterranean Lamb Chops + Stuffed Peppers with Rice and Vegetables	Greek Yogurt Parfait
16	Mediterranean Breakfast Wrap	Mediterranean Chickpea Stew + Greek Salad	Baked Greek Cod with Lemon and Herbs + Mediterranean Couscous Salad	Labneh with Honey and Pistachios
17	Shakshuka	Mediterranean Bulgur Salad + Tzatziki Sauce	Greek Lemon Garlic Chicken + Roasted Garlic Tomato Bruschetta	Mediterranean Scrambled Eggs (sweet version)

18	Greek Oatmeal with Honey and Walnuts	Mediterranean Quinoa Salad + Hummus	Mediterranean Beef Skewers + Greek-style Green Beans	Greek Yogurt Parfait
19	Mediterranean Breakfast Burrito	Mediterranean Vegetarian Wrap + Baba Ganush	Grilled Shrimp with Lemon and Garlic + Roasted Mediterranean Vegetables	Mediterranean Breakfast Wrap (sweet version)
20	Turkish Menemen	Greek Lentil Soup + Tabuli Salad	Moroccan Fish and Chickpea Tagine + Mediterranean Rice Pilaf	Labneh with Honey and Pistachios
21	Mediterranean Avocado Toast	Greek Chicken Pita Souvlaki + Mediterranean Chickpea Salad	Spanish Chicken and Chorizo Paella + Greek Roast Potatoes	Mediterranean Scrambled Eggs (sweet version)
22	Labneh with Honey and Pistachios	Mediterranean Couscous with Chickpeas + Tzatziki Sauce	Grilled Mediterranean Salmon + Roasted Eggplant with Tahini	Greek Yogurt Parfait
23	Mediterranean Omelet	Mediterranean Bulgur Salad + Hummus	Greek Lemon Garlic Chicken + Mediterranean Rice and Beans	Mediterranean Breakfast Wrap (with a sweet twist)
24	Breakfast Quesadilla with Feta and Spinach	Mediterranean Chickpea Stew + Baba Ganush	Grilled Shrimp with Lemon and Garlic + Greek Lemon Roasted Potatoes	Labneh with Honey and Pistachios
25	Mediterranean Avocado Toast	Mediterranean White Bean Salad + Greek Salad	Mediterranean Italian Sea Bass + Greek-style Green Beans	Greek Yogurt Parfait
26	Turkish Menemen	Greek Pastitsio + Marinated Olives	Spanish Seafood Paella + Mediterranean Roasted Red Peppers	Mediterranean Breakfast Burrito (with a sweet twist)
27	Spanakopita Breakfast Casserole	Mediterranean Tuna Salad +	Greek Moussaka with Ground Meat + Tomato	Labneh with Honey and Pistachios

		Stuffed Grape Leaves (Dolmas)	and Cucumber Salad	
28	Breakfast Frittata with Olives and Tomato	Mediterranean Vegetarian Wrap + Hummus	Moroccan Chicken Tagine + Mediterranean Zucchini Fritters	Greek Yogurt Parfait
29	Mediterranean Breakfast Burrito	Greek Lentil Soup + Tabuli Salad	Grilled Turkish Octopus + Mediterranean Couscous Salad	Fresh Fruit with a Drizzle of Honey and a Sprinkle of Chopped Nuts
30	Shakshuka	Mediterranean Quinoa Salad + Baba Ganush	Greek Fisherman Stew + Greek Roasted Eggplant Salad	Baked Pears with Honey and Walnuts
31	Mediterranean Scrambled Eggs	Mediterranean White Bean Salad + Stuffed Grape Leaves (Dolmas)	Baked Mediterranean Tilapia + Mediterranean Roasted Vegetables	Greek Yogurt with Sliced Fruits and a Drizzle of Honey
32	Greek Oatmeal with Honey and Walnuts	Mediterranean Chickpea Salad + Tzatziki Sauce	Tunisian Fish Tagine + Sautéed Kale with Lemon and Garlic	Poached Figs in Honey and Lemon Syrup
33	Mediterranean Avocado Toast	Greek Chicken Pita Souvlaki + Humus	Grilled Mediterranean Lamb Chops + Mediterranean Rice Pilaf	Baklava
34	Labneh with Honey and Pistachios	Mediterranean Bulgur Salad + Baba Ganush	Greek Lemon Garlic Chicken + Roasted Beet Salad with Feta Cheese	Honeyed Greek Yogurt with Pistachios and Rosewater
35	Mediterranean Omelet	Pasta with Mediterranean Tomato Sauce + Greek Salad	Mediterranean Beef Skewers + Grilled Mediterranean Vegetables	Pomegranate and Orange Salad with a Drizzle of Honey
36	Quinoa for Mediterranean Breakfast	Mediterranean Grilled Cheese + Roasted	Moroccan Lamb Stew + Greek	Olive Tapenade spread over light

		Mediterranean Vegetables	Roasted Eggplant Salad	crackers with a drizzle of honey
37	Spanakopita Breakfast Casserole	Grilled Eggplant and Halloumi Sandwich + Baba Ganush	Spanish Chicken and Chorizo Paella + Sautéed Kale with Lemon and Garlic	Labneh Sauce with fresh berries and a sprinkle of crushed pistachios
38	Greek Oatmeal with Honey and Walnuts	Mediterranean Chickpea Salad + Tzatziki Sauce	Grilled Turkish Octopus + Mediterranean Rice Pilaf	Avgolemono Greek Sauce (sweetened) served as a light custard
39	Mediterranean Breakfast Wrap	Pita and Falafel Sandwich + Mediterranean Red Pepper Sauce	Grilled Mediterranean Lamb Chops + Roasted Beet Salad with Feta Cheese	Sweetened Mediterranean Pesto with sliced almonds and fresh mint on puff pastry
40	Mediterranean Scrambled Eggs	Mediterranean Vegetarian Quesadilla + Greek Salad Dressing (as a dip)	Baked Mediterranean Tilapia + Mediterranean Couscous with Chickpeas	Romesco Sauce chocolate truffles (Romesco mixed with chocolate for a nutty treat)
41	Mediterranean Breakfast Burrito	Greek Chicken Pita Souvlaki + Tabuli Salad	Turkish Kofte (Spiced Meatballs) + Greek-style Green Beans	Mediterranean Sauce sweetened with figs and served with toast
42	Mediterranean Breakfast Pizza	Mediterranean Vegetarian Pizza + Marinated Olives	Grilled Sicilian Sardines + Stuffed Peppers with Rice and Vegetables	Sweet Tahini Sauce drizzled over fresh fruit salad
43	Greek Yogurt Parfait	Mediterranean Flatbread Pizza + Stuffed Grape Leaves (Dolmas)	Mediterranean Italian Pork Chops + Mediterranean Chickpea Salad	Honey and Walnut Quinoa (a sweet twist on Quinoa for Mediterranean Breakfast)

44	Mediterranean Avocado Toast	Mediterranean Rice Pilaf + Falafel	Lebanese Chicken Shawarma + Roasted Garlic Tomato Bruschetta	Greek Salad with Honey Dressing (a sweet twist on Greek Salad)
45	Turkish Menemen	Mediterranean White Bean Salad + Broad Bean Dip (Foul Mudammas)	Grilled Mediterranean Vegetables + Tomato and Olive Farro Salad	Pita Chips with Sweetened Hummus
46	Mediterranean Breakfast Burrito	Mediterranean Tuna Wrap + Mediterranean Couscous Salad	Baked Greek Cod with Lemon and Herbs + Greek Roasted Eggplant Salad	Labneh Sauce with Fresh Fruits
47	Breakfast Frittata with Olives and Tomato	Mediterranean Bulgur Salad + Mediterranean Chickpea Stew	Grilled Mediterranean Salmon + Sautéed Kale with Lemon and Garlic	Baba Ganush with Pomegranate Molasses
48	Spanakopita Breakfast Casserole	Mediterranean Quinoa Salad + Greek Gyro Sandwich	Baked Mediterranean Tilapia + Greek Lemon Roasted Potatoes	Sweetened Tahini Sauce Drizzled over Grilled Pineapple
49	Shakshuka	Mediterranean Rice and Beans + Mediterranean Pesto	Mediterranean Pork Souvlaki + Roasted Mediterranean Vegetables	Greek Salad Dressing as a Dip for Fresh Fruits
50	Labneh with Honey and Pistachios	Greek Lentil Soup + Fat Salad	Greek Lemon Garlic Chicken + Mediterranean Roasted Red Peppers	Fresh Fruit with a Drizzle of Harissa Sauce (sweetened)
51	Mediterranean Omelet	Pasta with Mediterranean Tomato Sauce + Marinated Olives	Moroccan Chicken Tagine + Tomato and Cucumber Salad	Greek Taramasalata (traditionally a savory dip, repurposed as a base for a

			savory-sweet dessert spread on biscuits)
52	Breakfast Quesadilla with Feta and Spinach	Spanakopita Greek Pasta + Stuffed Peppers with Rice and Vegetables	Grilled Mediterranean Lamb Chops + Greek-style Green Bean	Romesco Sauce over Vanilla Ice Cream
53	Mediterranean Scrambled Eggs	Greek Pastitsio + Roasted Beet Salad with Feta Cheese	Grilled Shrimp with Lemon and Garlic + Greek Roast Potatoes	Avgolemono Sauce mixed with Yogurt (for a tangy dessert)
54	Breakfast Frittata with Olives and Tomato	Mediterranean Chickpea Stew + Roasted Eggplant with Tahini	Tunisian Fish Tagine + Greek-style Green Beans	Olive Tapenade and Mascarpone on Toasted Brioche
55	Mediterranean Breakfast Wrap	Lebanese Mujadara + Greek Roasted Eggplant Salad	Greek Moussaka with Ground Meat + Mediterranean Zucchini Fritters	Chermoula Mixed with Honey and Served with Phyllo Pastry
56	Mediterranean Avocado Toast	Mediterranean Bulgur Salad + Greek Lemon Roasted Potatoes	Greek Fisherman's Stew + Roasted Garlic Tomato Bruschetta	Labneh Sauce Sweetened with Honey and Served with Fruit
57	Shakshuka	Mediterranean Couscous with Chickpeas + Grilled Mediterranean Vegetables	Italian Mediterranean Meatballs + Sautéed Kale with Lemon and Garlic	Greek Salad Dressing Sweetened as a Fruit Dip
58	Greek Oatmeal with Honey and Walnuts	Mediterranean White Bean Salad + Mediterranean Roasted Red Peppers	Greek-style Grilled Steak + Roasted Beet Salad with Feta Cheese	Harissa Sauce Sweetened and Mixed into Cream Cheese, Spread over Crackers
59	Mediterranean Breakfast Bowl	Mediterranean Rice and Beans + Grilled	Moroccan Lamb Stew + Mushrooms	Sweetened Baba Ganush with Sliced Apples

		Eggplant and Halloumi Sandwich	Stuffed with Greek Spinach and Feta Cheese	
60	Mediterranean Avocado Toast	Mediterranean White Bean Salad + Greek Stuffed Squid	Spanish seafood paella + Stuffed Peppers with Rice and Vegetables	Tahini Sauce sweetened and spread over figs or dates

Kitchen Measurement Abbreviations (Standard and Metric)

Abbreviation	Measurement
tbsp	tablespoon
tsp	teaspoon
oz	ounce
fl. oz	fluid ounce
c	cup
qt	quart
pt	pint
gal	gallon
lb	pound
mL	milliliter
g	grams
kg	kilogram
l	liter

Dry Measurements Conversion Chart

Teaspoons	Tablespoons	Cups
3 tsp	1 tbsp	1/16 c
6 tsp	2 tbsp	1/8 c
12 tsp	4 tbsp	1/4 c
24 tsp	8 tbsp	1/2 c
36 tsp	12 tbsp	3/4 c
48 tsp	16 tbsp	1 c

Liquid Measurements Conversion Chart

Fluid Ounces	Cups	Pints	Quarts	Gallons
8 fl. oz	1 c	1/2 pt	1/4 qt	1/16 gal
16 fl. oz	2 c	1 pt	1/2 qt	1/8 gal
32 fl. oz	4 c	2 pt	1 qt	1/4 gal
64 fl. oz	8 c	4 pt	2 qt	1/2 gal
128 fl. oz	16 c	8 pt	4 qt	1 gal

Butter Measurements Chart

Sticks	Cups	Tablespoons	Ounces	Grams
1/2 stick	1/4 c	4 tbsp	2 oz	57.5 g
1 stick	1/2 c	8 tbsp	4 oz	115 g
2 sticks	1 c	16 tbsp	8 oz	230 g

Oven Temperatures Conversion

(Degrees) Celsius	(Degrees) Fahrenheit
120 C	250 F
160 C	320 F
180 C	350 F
205 C	400 F
220 C	425 F

Weight Equivalents US Standard Metric (approximate)

½ ounce	15 g
1 ounce	30 g
2 ounces	60 g
4 ounces	115 g
8 ounces	225 g
12 ounces	340 g

DOWNLOAD YOUR FREE BONUS

SCAN ME

Printed in Great Britain
by Amazon

38542217R00064